CW00661970

Five Go Feasting

Enid Blyton®

First published in Great Britain in 2018 by Seven Dials
An imprint of Orion Publishing Group Ltd
Carmelite House, 50 Victoria Embankment, London, EC4Y 0DZ

An Hachette UK Company

10 9 8 7 6 5 4 3 2 1

Text by Josh Sutton
Original illustrations by Eileen Soper
Cover illustration by Ruth Palmer
Additional inside illustrations by Emanuel Santos

A CIP catalogue record for this book is available from the British Library.

Hardback ISBN: 9781841883304
Ebook ISBN: 9781841883311

Printed and bound by CPI Group (UK) Ltd, Croydon, CR0 4YY

www.orionbooks.co.uk

FIVE GO FEASTING

Josh Sutton

Quotations from

FAMOUSLY GOOD RECIPES

SEVEN DIALS

Contents

Introduction

'They decided to ask their aunt the next day if they might go and spend the weekend at the castle. The weather was gloriously fine, and it would be great fun. They could take plenty of food with them.'
(FIVE ON A TREASURE ISLAND)

WITH THEIR APPETITE FOR adventure, matched equally by an appetite for a jolly good feast, the tales of the Famous Five continue to delight both children and parents, generation after generation. The Five first came together in 1942 when Julian, Dick and Anne went to stay with their cousin George and Timmy the dog at Kirrin Cottage. In telling the tale of a group of new friends setting off for Kirrin Island, laden with two kitbags of camping equipment and enough food to feed a small army, author Enid Blyton managed to capture an essence of childhood that has stood the test of time. *Five on a Treasure Island* was the first in a series of twenty-one ripping adventures, which were published annually between 1942 and 1963, in which Julian, Dick, Anne, George and Timmy saw off smugglers, kidnappers, spies, thieves and a whole host of other rogues, villains and ne'er-do-wells.

Enid Blyton's capacity for enthralling her readers emerged from her clear understanding of the inquisitive nature of children, their sense of adventure and in-built yearning for excitement. But part of the success of the Famous Five series is also due to the author's understanding of the importance of food in recounting a good yarn. Her capacity for describing farmhouse breakfasts and delicious picnics has meant that, over the years, the Famous Five gained notoriety not just for their sense of derring-do, but as true gourmands also. Throughout nearly all of the adventures, food plays a central role in marking the day, particularly interesting and revealing as the first twelve books were written when food was rationed in Britain during and after the Second World War. In each story, careful thought is always given to what food is available and where the children might pick up supplies. And while it's the sensible and polite Julian who nearly always pays for any food bought from farmhouses and village shopkeepers, and Timmy the dog often gets to lick the plates clean, it is not just the foodstuff itself that is particularly redolent of the period in which the books were written. Tellingly, it is always poor Anne who takes up the role of keeping house and doing the washing-up.

'"George and I will get you a meal," said Anne. "We called at the farm on our way up and got a lovely lot of food. Come on, George." George got up unwillingly.'
(FIVE GO OFF IN A CARAVAN)

The food that the children eat is typical of the era in which the books were written: hams, pies, eggs, salad, home-grown fruit and ginger beer, of course. At that time, many of these foods would have been readily available, but, thanks to rationing, certainly not in the quantities that the children devour them. Interestingly, Enid Blyton doesn't write of exotic herbs, spices and foodstuffs, which were beginning to make their way into recipe books by the 1950s; she describes ingredients wholly familiar to those reading the stories at that time. Accounts of crisp lettuces, dewy and cool with golden hearts, and lashings of hard-boiled eggs, leave readers both young and old hungry for more.

Food rationing in Britain finally ended in 1954 but it was a time when food was scarce, and this made the feasts described all the more appealing. Tinned tuna and pineapple rings were perhaps the most exotic things the children came across. There were certainly no bananas. Yet the fact that so many of the meals that the Five eat, with the possible exception of tongue, are as popular today as when Blyton was writing is one of the reasons the stories continue to be read and enjoyed.

'"The thing is – can we possibly find food enough for so long? Even if we entirely empty the larder I doubt if that would be enough for a week or so. We all seem such hungry people, somehow."'
(FIVE RUN AWAY TOGETHER)

Food was so important to the Famous Five that in the third book of the series, *Five Run Away Together,* it's the poor performance of the temporary kitchen staff that sends them off on their adventure. The 'sour-faced' Mrs Stick, who temporarily replaces Joanna as the cook at Kirrin Cottage, takes an instant dislike to the children and especially Timmy, their dog. In other adventures it's Joanna, the regular cook, who looks after the majority of the children's dietary needs, constantly supplying them with hamper after hamper of delicious goodies. At Dick's behest, Joanna is awarded the OBCBE – 'order of the best cook of the British Empire' – following yet another escapade in *Five on Kirrin Island Again*. As well as an abundance of sweet treats, cakes and gallons of lemonade and ginger beer, the children also consume huge amounts of fresh fruit, salad and vegetables. The pies that they eat are all home-made and additive-free. This was an age before processed food really took off, well before today's factory-farming methods and the might of the supermarkets. All in all, the Famous Five enjoyed a healthy diet, one that was fitting for the sheer amount of exercise and energy expended in living their childhood outside in the open countryside.

Joanna's kitchen bookshelves would have been brimming with contemporary cookbook authors: Mrs Beeton surely taking pride of place next to Mary Ronald, Elizabeth Craig, Nancy Lake and Marguerite Patten. Later, as rationing ended, new cookery writers, possibly Ambrose Heath or Philip Harben, may have found their way onto the shelves as this next generation of writers helped teach Britain to cook. Elizabeth David's championing of European cuisine may have been a little too exotic for Joanna, though.

The food environment in post-war Britain, when the majority of the series was written, was witness to immeasurable change. Farms grew in size, partly because the demand for crops during the war years had dictated it, but also because new technology made harvesting much easier and more efficient. New innovations in food preservation and storage meant that increasingly exotic ingredients were finding their way onto grocery shelves. The re-established transport networks after the war would have brought bananas and other tropical fruits back to our shores, but Enid Blyton sticks happily with the familiar.

'How lovely to wake in a strange place at the beginning of a holiday, to think of bathing and biking and picnicking and eating and drinking, forgetting all about exams and rules and punishments!'
(FIVE GO DOWN TO THE SEA)

Five Go Feasting will help you capture the magic of the Famous Five books, possibly revisiting your own childhood through these eighty recipes, all inspired by the meals that Julian, Dick, George and Anne enjoyed throughout their adventures. Where possible, the recipes adhere faithfully to the food environment of the time, without the use of complex exotic ingredients. So, in some ways, this menu is like a journey back in time, back to a world where an appreciation of simple, basic ingredients far outweighed the desire for mass-produced processed food.

Nowadays, when children are spending more time indoors staring at screens than playing outdoors, it seems all the more important to celebrate and remember this group of five fictional friends, whose love of adventure and the English countryside has brought joy to generations of would-be sleuths and adventurers. We might just learn a thing or two, and with any luck may even be tempted to slip on our galoshes, grab a knapsack full of scrummy sandwiches and disappear out into the big wide open. We will, of course, be back in time for a huge slap-up tea of cream cakes and ginger beer.

'They had breakfast and ate just as much as ever'
(FIVE ON A TREASURE ISLAND)

Chapter One

A Jolly Good Breakfast

Porridge & Cream

SERVES 4

'"Porridge and cream,' said the woman. "And our own cured bacon and our own eggs. Our own honey and the bread I baked myself. Will that do? And coffee with cream?"
"I could hug you," said Julian, beaming at her.'
(FIVE ON A HIKE TOGETHER)

It was either Napoleon or Frederick the Great who remarked that an army marches on its stomach, and clearly it was a phrase taken to heart by Julian, Dick, Anne and George. As they set off in *Five on a Hike Together*, it was a hearty helping of porridge and cream that set them on their way.

160g rolled porridge oats
700ml semi-skimmed or skimmed milk
200ml double cream
4 tsp golden syrup (optional – but not if you're Julian!)

Place the oats and milk in a saucepan and bring to a simmer for 5–6 minutes, stirring with a wooden spoon. As the porridge thickens, pour out into bowls and serve with a little cream and a spoonful of golden syrup, if you like.

Eggy Bread

SERVES 2

With so many eggs eaten by the Famous Five, we can only guess at how all of them were cooked. Here's a great breakfast recipe that will get you up and out into the countryside in no time. While our heroes might not have had the luxury of maple syrup, there's no reason you shouldn't.

4 free-range eggs
flaky sea salt and freshly ground black pepper
a little milk
4 slices bread
vegetable oil, for frying
maple syrup, to serve

Crack the eggs into a jug and add a splash of milk, a pinch of sea salt and a little black pepper. Whisk well with a fork and pour into a shallow bowl. Coat both sides of the bread in the egg mixture. Warm a glug of oil in a non-stick frying pan and fry the eggy bread for 2–3 minutes on each side.

Serve hot with a dribble of maple syrup.

'They sat down in the heather and began their breakfast. Anne fried big rounds of bread in the fat, and the boys told her she was the best cook in the world.'
(FIVE GO OFF TO CAMP)

Bacon & Eggs with tomato & fried bread

SERVES 2

The Five always manage to start the day on a fine breakfast, and this feast of bacon and eggs would set them up for many adventures.

knob of lard or splash of vegetable oil
4 rashers dry-cured smoky bacon
2 tomatoes, halved
2 free-range eggs
2 slices white bread

Preheat the oven to its lowest temperature and warm three plates inside.

Melt the lard, or heat the oil, in a large frying pan over a moderate heat. Add the bacon and, once it begins to curl, turn it over and move to one side of the pan. Next add the tomatoes to the pan, cut side down. Keep turning the bacon as it begins to brown and the tomatoes cook.

Make space in the pan and crack in the eggs and fry them gently until cooked. Remove the bacon, eggs and tomatoes and transfer to a warmed plate.

Turn up the heat and fry the slices of bread quickly in the fat in the pan, turning once after a minute or two, as they soak up all the flavour. Once the bread crisps up, serve on the remaining warmed plates, topped with the other ingredients.

Warm Toasted Crumpets

MAKES 8

It's all too easy to tear a couple of crumpets from a packet and sling them in the toaster, but they're far nicer when made fresh – just as the Famous Five would have had then.

250ml water
250ml milk
1 tsp sugar
1 tbsp vegetable oil, plus extra for greasing
15g dried active yeast
1 tbsp salt
450g flour (225g strong white and 225g plain)
½ tsp bicarbonate of soda
salted butter, for spreading

YOU WILL NEED
griddle pan
4 crumpet rings

Combine the water, milk, sugar and oil in a saucepan and warm very gently over a low heat for just a minute. Remove from the heat and stir in the yeast.

Add the salt to the flour and sift into the liquid, stirring and beating to form a batter. Cover the batter with a tea towel and leave to rise for at least an hour.

Beat the risen batter down with a wooden spoon and stir in the bicarbonate of soda dissolved in 300ml warm water. Mix thoroughly and set aside for 30 minutes.

Grease the griddle pan and crumpet rings. Place the rings in the griddle pan and half fill each ring with batter until almost full. Cook very gently over a moderate heat until the air bubbles form numerous tiny holes over the top surface of the crumpets. This should take around 10 minutes. Using a pair of tongs and taking care not to burn your fingers, remove the crumpets from the rings, flip them over and cook the upper (holey) side for a further 2–3 minutes. Repeat to make another 4 crumpets. Serve fresh with butter.

Dippy Egg & Soldiers

SERVES 2

Boiled eggs are one of the most frequently featured foods in all of the Five's adventures. Hard-boiled, they show up in salads, in sandwiches, and of course eaten whole with a sprinkle of salt. There were, in fact, lashings of hard-boiled eggs throughout the series. Soft-boiled, dippy eggs are always eaten at breakfast with toast.

2 slices bread
salted butter, for spreading
2 fresh free-range eggs

Toast the bread, then butter and cut each slice into thin strips for dunking into the eggs.

Place the eggs in a small saucepan and cover with cold water. Bring to the boil. Boil vigorously for 2½ minutes. Drain away the hot water and serve immediately with the toast 'soldiers'. Remove the top of the eggs quickly to keep the yolks soft.

To hard-boil an egg, place it in a small saucepan of water, bring to the boil then simmer for 5 minutes. Pour the water away and replace with cold. Allow the egg to cool before peeling.

Boiled Tongue

SERVES 5

'They had a fine breakfast of tongue, tinned peaches, bread and butter, golden syrup and ginger beer.'
(FIVE RUN AWAY TOGETHER)

Possibly the least tempting dish on the entire menu throughout the series, boiled tongue nevertheless gets a mention in three of the stories and is usually devoured between slices of buttered white bread. Mrs Beeton advises choosing a tongue with a smooth skin as this means it's young and tender.

1 salted ox tongue
1 large onion
2 carrots
2 leeks
2 celery sticks
12 whole black peppercorns
2 bay leaves
1 rosemary sprig
buttered bread, to serve

Place the tongue in a large stockpot and cover amply with water.

Halve the onion, leaving the skin on, and add to the pot. Chop the remaining vegetables roughly and place in the pot along with the peppercorns and the herbs. Cover and bring to the boil. Turn down to a gentle simmer and cook with the lid on for 3 hours.

Remove the tongue from the stock and allow to cool a little. Peel away the skin and discard it, while the tongue is still warm. Serve cold and sliced thinly into a sandwich.

'"Oooh lovely," said Anne. "And you've done the sausages just how I like them, Joanna – all bursting their skins. Do you think we better eat George's too? She's still out in the boat. She may not be back for ages."'
(FIVE FALL INTO ADVENTURE)

Sausage Sandwiches

SERVES 2

Alongside eggs, sausages are a favourite throughout the stories. The sausages made under rationing, during the war, were very often bulked out with rusk in a bid to make what little meat was available go much further. Luckily, that's not so much the case these days. Who doesn't love a sausage sandwich?

dash vegetable oil
4 good-quality pork sausages
butter, for spreading
4 slices fresh white bread
brown sauce or ketchup

Put the oil in a frying pan and fry the sausages over a medium heat until they are brown all over, or until the skin splits if you so wish – 8 minutes or so should do the trick, depending on how fat your sausages are.

While the sausages are cooking, butter the bread slices. Once the bangers are cooked, remove from the heat and turn out onto a piece of kitchen paper. Carefully slice them in two lengthways and build your sandwich – two sausages to a sandwich, flat side down on the bread. Top with either red or brown sauce and devour. If your friend is still out in the boat, you can eat theirs too.

Stewed Rhubarb

SERVES 4

Much has changed since Enid Blyton first began writing the Famous Five books back in the 1940s, in particular our use of language. 'Stewed fruit' belongs to a bygone era; we call it compote these days, but it still tastes just as good on our breakfast cereal. Or even as a dessert, served with vanilla custard.

500g rhubarb
50ml orange juice
100g golden caster sugar

Top and tail the rhubarb and cut into 1cm chunks. Place in a large lidded saucepan together with the orange juice. Simmer with the lid on for 10 minutes, or until the rhubarb begins to soften and break down.

Add the sugar, stir and simmer gently for a further 5 minutes. Add a little water if the fruit becomes too dry. This will keep in the fridge for 3–4 days.

Strawberry Jam

MAKES 4 × 450g JARS

It sits on toast, on scones with clotted cream, in tarts and in Victoria sponges. Jam is so easy to make and, especially towards the end of the strawberry season (early July) when prices tumble, it is very cost-effective to boot.

1kg strawberries
1kg preserving sugar
juice of 1 lemon

YOU WILL NEED
preserving pan or the biggest, widest pan you own
4 sterilised jars (see page 26)

Wash, hull and quarter the strawberries and place them in a preserving pan with the sugar and lemon juice. Heat slowly while mashing the sugar into the strawberries with a wooden spoon. Once all the sugar has dissolved, bring to a rolling boil for about 10 minutes until setting point is reached. Setting point test: drop a spoonful of jam onto a cold plate and allow to cool. Push it with your finger and if the jam ripples then it's ready to put into jars.

Pour the jam into sterilised jars and seal immediately. Unopened, this jam will keep for up to a year.

Orange Marmalade

MAKES 6 × 450g JARS

No breakfast table is complete without an open jar of marmalade to pass around. It's easy to make, and best with Seville oranges which are available from late January through to the end of February. The 1934 recipe by Elizabeth Craig, a notable cookery writer of the time, serves as the basis for this simple orange marmalade, but upping the sugar content and adding a lemon vastly improves it.

1kg (roughly 6–8) Seville oranges
1 lemon
2.5 litres water
2kg sugar

Remove the peel and cut it into thin shreds. Simmer the peel in a litre of the water for 30 minutes. Meanwhile, remove as much of the pith from the peeled fruit as possible, then chop the flesh roughly and simmer in a pan with the remainder of the water for 30 minutes. Strain the resulting juice through a fine sieve.

Put the juice, sugar and shredded peel plus cooking water in a large saucepan. Bring to the boil and cook for about 15 minutes until the setting point has been reached. Setting point test: pour a teaspoon of the marmalade onto a chilled plate and allow to cool for 1 minute. Push the surface. If it wrinkles it has reached setting point.

Allow the marmalade to cool a little, then pour into sterilised jars* and seal immediately. The marmalade will keep well for a year (not that it will last that long!).

* To sterilise jars, wash them thoroughly in soapy water, rinse and place on a baking tray in the oven at 180°C/fan 160°C/350°F/gas 4 for 15–20 minutes.

'Downstairs breakfast awaited them. "Super!" said Dick, eyeing the bacon and fried eggs, the cold ham, and the home-made jam and marmalade. "Mrs Penruthlan, your seven children must have been very sorry to marry and leave home. I feel, if I'd been one of them, I'd have stayed with you for the rest of my life!"'
(FIVE GO DOWN TO THE SEA)

'They picnicked on the sands with Timothy sharing more than half their lunch'
(FIVE GO DOWN TO THE SEA)

Chapter Two

PERFECT PICNICS

Home-cooked Ham

SERVES LOTS! (OR 4 FOR DINNER)

It's safe to say that ham forms a mainstay of the Famous Five's diet. Ham sandwiches, ham salad, cold roast ham with potatoes, the list goes on. So a recipe for a home-cooked ham is essential if you are to feast like the Famous Five. This cooked ham would make a dozen sandwiches with some left over for the dog.

1kg dry-cured, free-range gammon joint
1 onion
2 celery sticks
4 star anise
12 whole black peppercorns

FOR THE GLAZE
handful of cloves
1 jar Orange Marmalade (see page 26)

Place the gammon joint in a large stockpot. Cover with water and bring to the boil. Pour away the water. This will remove much of the salt used in the dry-cure process.

Halve the onion, skin on, and chop the celery. Throw them in the pot along with the star anise and peppercorns. Pour in enough water to cover the joint by at least 7cm. Bring to the boil and simmer with a lid on for 1 hour.

After the ham has been boiling for about 50 minutes, preheat the oven to 180°C/fan 160°C/350°F/gas 4.

Remove the joint from the stockpot and pat dry with kitchen paper. Next, remove the skin, but leave as thick a layer of fat on the joint as possible. Now stud the ham with as many cloves as you like and cover entirely with orange marmalade. Place in a roasting dish and cook in the oven for about 20 minutes until the outside is a lovely deep golden brown colour. Allow to rest for at least 30 minutes before carving.

'"We've got a marvellous piece of boiled ham – look! It'll last us for ages – if we don't give bits to Timmy. Get away, Tim. This is not for you! Grrrrrr!"'
(FIVE ON A SECRET TRAIL)

Anchovy Paste

MAKES 1 × 120g JAR

'They had tea about half-past five, and then bought what they wanted for supper and breakfast. New rolls, anchovy paste, a big round jam tart in a cardboard box, oranges, lime-juice, a fat lettuce and some ham sandwiches – it seemed a very nice assortment indeed.'
(FIVE GET INTO TROUBLE)

Anchovy paste is a great flavour enhancer. Spread very thinly on a ham sandwich, it lifts it to another level.

1 garlic clove
120g re-sealable jar anchovy fillets
freshly ground black pepper
½ tsp white wine vinegar
½ tsp olive oil

YOU WILL NEED
pestle and mortar

Peel the garlic and crush to a paste in a pestle and mortar. Remove the anchovies from the jar and drain, discarding the oil but retaining the jar. Add the anchovies to the crushed garlic along with a good grind of black pepper, the vinegar and olive oil. Grind to a paste in the pestle and mortar and replace into the anchovy jar.

Potted Meat

MAKES ABOUT 500g

'"We'd love to have you stay," said Anne in delight. "I'll cut some bread and butter and make some sandwiches. Do you like potted meat sandwiches, Nobby?"'
(FIVE GO OFF IN A CARAVAN)

Potted meat is a very English version of what the French might call pâté. Spread thickly between two slices of crusty white bread, it makes for a very filling sandwich.

variety of cooked meats – pork, beef, lamb (about 400g total weight)
knob of butter
salt and freshly ground black pepper
splash of Worcestershire sauce
1 tsp Anchovy Paste *(see page 32)*
1 tbsp double cream
100g butter, for sealing

YOU WILL NEED
pâté dish

Place the scraps of cooked meat in a food processor along with all the ingredients except the butter. Blitz to a paste and spread into a pâté dish.

Melt the butter and pour over the top of the meat paste to form a seal. Refrigerate for an hour before serving. The potted meat will keep for three or four days in the fridge.

A Loaf of 'New Bread'

MAKES 1 LARGE LOAF

'Once again they bought food for their lunch – new bread, farmhouse butter, cream cheese, crisp lettuce, fat red radishes and a bunch of spring onions.'
(FIVE GET INTO TROUBLE)

There is simply nothing quite like the smell of bread baking in an oven. Time after time, Enid Blyton mentions fresh baked 'new bread' in the Famous Five stories. There's nearly always a loaf on every farmhouse kitchen table.

500g strong white bread flour
1 packet of active yeast
1 tsp salt
1 tbsp honey
300ml tepid water

Combine all of the ingredients in a large bowl and mix to a soft dough. Turn the dough out onto a floured surface and knead using the base of your palm for ten minutes until the dough is smooth and elastic. Return to the mixing bowl, cover with a damp tea towel and leave to prove for an hour until roughly doubled in size.

Ten minutes before you're ready to bake the bread, pre-heat the oven to 200°C.

Place the risen dough on a lightly floured surface and shape to form a loaf. Place on a greased baking sheet and make three or four diagonal slashes across the top of the loaf. Cover with a dry tea towel and leave to prove for a further half hour then place in the hot oven and bake for 30 minutes until the crust is golden.

Sardine Sandwiches

SERVES 2

A sardine sandwich on anything other than a crusty roll just won't work. You'll end up with a soggy mess that might be just fine for Timmy the dog, but will never do for aspiring adventurers.

2 large crusty rolls
butter, for spreading
120g tin of sardines
salt and freshly ground black pepper
squeeze of fresh lemon juice (optional)

Split the rolls and spread with butter. Open the sardine tin, fork out the fish and spread evenly over the bottom half of each roll. Season with salt and pepper and a drop of lemon juice if you like. Place the top on and tuck in.

Tuna Sandwiches

SERVES 2

Tuna is one of the most exotic foods to find its way into Anne's picnic hamper. In Britain today, tuna is second only to salmon as the most consumed fish. It doesn't make an appearance on the Famous Five's menu until the penultimate adventure when *Five Have a Mystery to Solve*. It's eaten straight from the tin and in a sandwich too. There's no mention of mayonnaise, but you can add it if you want to.

butter, for spreading
4 slices bread
160g tin of tuna
freshly ground black pepper
mayonnaise (optional)

Butter the bread. Fork the tuna straight from the tin onto two of the slices of bread. Season with black pepper to taste and add a dollop of mayo if you like. Top with the remaining slices and cut diagonally.

"'Now you've made me want my lunch all the more – talking about egg sandwiches and ginger beer! I know Mother made us egg sandwiches – and sardine ones too.'"
(FIVE GET INTO TROUBLE)

Egg Sandwiches

SERVES 2

The egg and cress sandwich in many ways typifies the great British picnic. The Famous Five certainly ate their way through one or two egg sandwiches, but they seemed to prefer lettuce to cress with theirs. Choose your own accompaniment.

2 hard-boiled eggs (see page 20)
2 tsp mayonnaise
salt and freshly ground black pepper
4 slices white bread
butter, for spreading
cress (or a couple of shredded lettuce leaves if you prefer)

Peel the eggs and mash together with the mayonnaise in a bowl. Season to taste. Spread the bread thinly with soft butter and apply liberal amounts of the egg mayonnaise. Top with a scattering of cut cress, place a slice of bread on top and cut diagonally.

Ham & Mustard Sandwiches

SERVES 2

The simple sandwich was a staple of the Famous Five's diet, with ham being a firm favourite. Best served on thickly sliced crusty farmhouse white bread with bright yellow English mustard and a lettuce leaf.

butter, for spreading
4 thick slices crusty bread
4 slices roast ham from your local butcher or cooked yourself (see page 30)
English mustard
a couple of crisp lettuce leaves

Spread a generous dollop of butter over the slices of bread. Divide the ham evenly over two slices of bread and spread a little English mustard on top. Add a lettuce leaf before closing off the sandwiches with the top slice of bread and cutting in half.

'"Cucumber, dipped in vinegar! Ham and lettuce! Egg! Sardine! Oooh, Mr Luffy, your sandwiches are much nicer than ours," said Anne, beginning on two together, one cucumber and the other ham and lettuce.'
(FIVE GO OFF TO CAMP)

Brawn

SERVES 6

Brawn is a classic dish of meat served in its own jelly. It fits well in times of austerity because it uses up all the parts of an animal. Here, and with a nod to English chef and food writer, Mark Hix, we use rabbit as well as a pig's trotter, which provides all the lovely gelatine to set the brawn. You'll be able to pick up a trotter from your local butcher.

1 pig's trotter
1 medium onion
1 leek
1 celery stick
2 garlic cloves
a few whole black peppercorns
1 bouquet garni
1 tsp salt
1 rabbit, jointed
toast, for serving

Place the pig's trotter, the vegetables roughly chopped, peppercorns and bouquet garni in a large stockpot and cover well with cold water. Add half the salt. Bring to the boil, and simmer gently for 1 hour.

Add the rabbit and a little water if the pot is looking dry. Continue to simmer for 45 minutes, or until the flesh of the rabbit falls easily away from the bone.

Strain the contents through a colander but retain the liquid. Pass the liquid through a fine sieve and pour into a medium saucepan. Heat the saucepan and boil to reduce in volume by about half. Taste for seasoning, adding the remaining salt if required. Allow to cool a little, but not to set.

Remove all of the meat from the bones of the rabbit and the trotter. Mix with the reduced liquid and pour into a terrine mould or suitable dish. Cover with clingfilm and, once cool, place in the fridge overnight to set completely. Slice thinly and serve on hot toast.

Radish & Spring Onion Salad

SERVES 4

The Five would most likely have eaten the hot, peppery radishes and the crunchy spring onions on their own, but combining the two with a dash of oil, mustard and fresh lime juice makes for a terrific quick salad.

200g radishes
1 bunch spring onions
1 tbsp olive oil
juice of ½ lime
½ tsp wholegrain mustard
salt and freshly ground black pepper

Top and tail the radishes and slice lengthways into three pieces. Place in a shallow dish. Top and tail the spring onions, quarter them lengthways and scatter in the dish with the radishes.

In a small cup or jug combine the olive oil, lime juice and mustard and pour over the onions and radishes. Turn through to coat the vegetables in the dressing and season to taste.

'Once again they bought food for their lunch – new bread, farmhouse butter, cream cheese, crisp lettuce, fat red radishes and a bunch of spring onions.'
(FIVE GET INTO TROUBLE)

Cold Meat Salad

SERVES 2

'They were all very hungry at lunch-time. They went back up the cliff-path, hoping there would be lots to eat – and there was! Cold meat and salad, plum-pie and custard, and cheese afterwards. How the children tucked in!'
(FIVE ON A TREASURE ISLAND)

Enid Blyton is not very specific when it comes to describing just what type of meat goes in a cold meat salad. Not that this makes much difference because, without a shadow of a doubt, the Famous Five would eat whatever was put in front of them, and then ask for a second helping. Cold chicken breast serves its purpose here.

2 small chicken breasts
juice of ½ lime (Joanna the cook might have used lemon juice)
sea salt and freshly ground black pepper
1 small cos lettuce
1 small red onion

You can use ready-cooked chicken breasts, or indeed cook them yourself. To cook them, season well and rub with a little oil. Place under a hot grill for 4 minutes, turn and cook the other side for a further 4 minutes. To check that they're cooked through, cut into one of the breasts and make sure the flesh is cooked white all the way through. Allow to cool before making the salad.

2 tsp plain yoghurt
2 tsp mayonnaise
50g croutons

Slice the chicken breasts and squeeze over the lime juice. Sprinkle with a pinch of sea salt and a good grind of black pepper.

Roughly chop the lettuce and throw into a salad bowl. Peel and halve the red onion, then slice very thinly. Add this to the bowl along with the yoghurt and mayonnaise, and mix thoroughly. Finally add the sliced chicken breast and the croutons, give it one more turn and serve.

Home-made Salad Cream

MAKES ROUGHLY 225ml

Salads are abundant in the Famous Five diet, and no salad would be complete without lashings of this fiery, unctuous dressing.

1 tbsp sugar
1 tsp salt
1 tsp plain flour
150ml milk
60g butter
1 egg
1 tsp English mustard
freshly ground black pepper
75ml malt vinegar

YOU WILL NEED
sterilised glass jar (see page 26)

Mix the dry ingredients together, along with a tablespoon of the milk, in a small jug.

Over a saucepan of simmering water, create a bain-marie by snugly fitting a glass bowl on top, making sure it doesn't touch the water. Melt the butter in the bain-marie and beat in the egg. Add in all of the other ingredients and stir continuously in the bain-marie until the sauce begins to thicken. Allow to cool thoroughly before use. Stored in a sterilised airtight jar it will keep in the fridge for a week or two.

Hard-boiled Egg Salad

SERVES 2

The sight of a few sliced hard-boiled eggs scattered across the top of a bowl of salad suggests a hearty meal in itself.

3 hard-boiled eggs (see page 20)
1 green lettuce
½ cucumber
2 tomatoes
4 spring onions
6 radishes
Home-made Salad Cream (see page 48)

Peel the eggs and halve them lengthways, then cut into quarters. Wash the lettuce leaves and put in a salad bowl with the eggs. Slice the cucumber, the tomatoes and the spring onions and scatter over the salad. Top and tail the radishes and halve them lengthways. Add these to the salad together with a dollop of salad cream. Turn through with a pair of salad servers and dig in.

Pork Pie

SERVES 4

"'It's a miracle," said Anne. "Just as I had made up my mind to starve for hours! A pork-pie of all things! Let's have some."'
(FIVE ON A HIKE TOGETHER)

Pork pie has been a picnic treat for generations. Here's how to make one for your own hamper.

FOR THE FILLING
300g minced pork shoulder
100g pork belly
fresh thyme sprig
1 sage leaf
freshly ground black pepper

FOR THE JELLY
1 pig's trotter
1 celery stick
6 whole black peppercorns
2 bay leaves
2 star anise
1 onion

FOR THE PASTRY
225g plain flour

Preheat the oven to 180°C/fan 160°C/350°F/gas 4.

To make the filling, put the minced pork in a bowl. Cut the belly pork into 1cm cubes and add to the bowl. Strip the thyme leaves from the stalk and chop the sage leaf, and add to the bowl with plenty of black pepper. Mix well with your hands and leave to stand while you prepare the jelly and make the pastry.

To make the jelly, halve the onion, skin on, and place all of the ingredients in a stockpot. Cover with water and bring to the boil. Simmer gently for 1 hour. Remove from the heat and strain through a sieve into a measuring jug. Reserve the liquid and discard the other ingredients.

For the pastry, combine the flour, salt and egg in a bowl. In a saucepan, bring the water and lard to the boil. Once the

pinch salt
1 egg
100ml water
75g lard
1 egg, beaten, for glazing

YOU WILL NEED
15cm pie dish

lard has melted pour the liquid into the bowl with the flour. Mix to a dough using a wooden spoon and, as soon as it is cool enough to handle, roll into a ball and allow to rest for a few minutes. Wrap the pastry in clingfilm and refrigerate for half an hour. Roll out the dough on a floured surface to line a circular pie dish, reserving a third of the mixture to make a lid.

Form the filling to a ball and place in the pie, pressing down gently but leaving space for the jelly to run through.

Roll out a pie lid and crimp the edges to seal to the sides. Make a small hole in the centre of the lid and place in the oven for 30 minutes. Remove from the oven and brush with the beaten egg to glaze. Lower the temperature to 170°C/fan 150°C/325°F/gas 3, and return the pie to the oven for a further 30 minutes until the crust is golden.

As soon as the pie is cooked, using a funnel, pour the jelly into the hole in the pie lid until it just overflows. Leave the pie to cool before eating, or refrigerate overnight if you want the jelly to set.

Farmhouse Pie

SERVES 4

A farmhouse pie is very much a dish of its time. During the rationing years, people were encouraged to eat more vegetables, particularly when the meat ration was low. This pie can be made with any vegetable you wish.

4 large King Edward potatoes
salt
2 knobs of butter
1 onion
1 leek
2 carrots
½ white cabbage
6 large runner beans
200ml water
½ tsp sugar
salt and freshly ground black pepper
3 tomatoes

Preheat the oven to 170°C/fan 150°C/325°F/gas 3.

Peel and quarter the potatoes. Boil in a large pan of salted water for around 5 minutes until the potatoes are soft. Drain and mash with a large knob of butter and a pinch of salt. Set aside.

Peel and chop the rest of the vegetables, except the tomatoes, and put them in a large saucepan with the water, sugar and remaining knob of butter. Cover with a tight-fitting lid and bring to the boil. Boil for 6 minutes then transfer the vegetables, with their cooking liquor, to a shallow heatproof dish. Season with salt and pepper.

Slice the tomatoes and arrange over the top of the vegetables. Form the mashed potato into small, flattened balls with your fingers. Arrange these across the top of the dish to cover. Place in the oven for 30 minutes until the potato browns on top.

Sausage Rolls

MAKES ABOUT 12

A sausage roll is a fine addition to any picnic. These simple snacks are so easy to make it would almost be a crime not to! For speed and ease, this recipe recommends using ready-made puff pastry, but it would also be a crime not to offer instruction on how to make your own.

450g ready-made puff pastry, or:
300g plain flour
200g butter, 50g cubed and 150g softened
juice of ½ lemon made up to 100ml with added water
450g pork sausage meat
salt and freshly ground black pepper
pinch dried mixed herbs
Worcestershire sauce
1 egg, beaten, for glazing

If making your own puff pastry try this quick recipe using softened butter.

Put the flour in a bowl and rub in the cubed butter until you have the consistency of breadcrumbs. Add enough of the lemon water (up to 5–6 tablespoons) until you are able to form a rough dough. Roll out the dough on a floured surface into a rectangle 5mm thick. Spread half of the softened butter evenly over the bottom two-thirds of the pastry and fold down the unbuttered top third and then fold up the bottom third. You now have three layers of pastry with butter sandwiched in between.

Next, turn the pastry through 90 degrees and roll out into another rectangle 5mm thick. Repeat the process with the remaining softened butter to make a total of six layers. Fold the dough in half and wrap it in clingfilm and refrigerate for at least 30 minutes before using.

Preheat the oven to 200°C/fan 180°C/400°F/gas 6.

Mix the sausagemeat thoroughly in a bowl together with some salt and pepper, the dried herbs and a glug of Worcestershire sauce.

Roll out the pastry, ready-made or home-made, to a thickness of no more than 5mm on a lightly floured surface and cut into two rectangles. Divide the sausagemeat in two and arrange along the middle of each of the rectangles. Fold the pastry over to form two long sausage rolls. Cut to preferred sizes, place on a baking tray and glaze with the beaten egg. Place in the oven for up to 15 minutes until the pastry is golden brown.

"'Anyone feel inclined to have dry bread and jam for lunch?" inquired Julian, when he returned to the others. "No? I rather thought so, so I turned down Mrs Stick's kind offer. I vote we go and buy something decent. That shop in the village has good sausage-rolls."'
(FIVE RUN AWAY TOGETHER)

Home-made Pickles

EACH RECIPE MAKES ABOUT TWO 500ml JARS

A spicy pickling vinegar lies at the heart of a tasty pickle. You can buy pickling vinegar off the shelf, but making your own is all part of the fun. Pickles, of course, were made as a means of preserving food in times of shortage and making sure that nothing gets wasted in the kitchen. The flavouring in the pickling vinegar can be varied with the addition of other spices at the boiling stage, such as blade mace, bruised ginger and cloves. Herbs such as dill can be added once the vinegar has cooled. Whole allspice is a fine addition for pickling beetroot.

FOR THE PICKLING VINEGAR

600ml clear malt vinegar
12 whole black peppercorns
1 tsp coriander seeds
2 tsp yellow mustard seeds
2 bay leaves
100g golden sugar

YOU WILL NEED:
2 x 500ml sterilised jars (see page 26)

Place all of the ingredients in a large saucepan and bring to the boil. Remove from the heat immediately and allow to cool slowly. Strain into a jug.

This will be enough to pickle any of the recipes set out below. You will need two 500ml sterilised jars in each case (see page 26).

Before immersing in pickling vinegar, most vegetables must be salted overnight to remove some of their moisture. In the recipes that follow, drain through a colander means simply that – drain away the majority of the salt liquid. Gently rub away any remaining salt with kitchen paper.

'"Don't tell us any more!" begged Dick. "It makes me feel too hungry. Why is it that people on farms always have the most delicious food? I mean, surely people in towns can bottle raspberries and pickle onions and make cream cheese?"'
(FIVE GO ON A HIKE TOGETHER)

FOR PICKLED RED CABBAGE

1 medium red cabbage
about 500ml pickling vinegar

Quarter the cabbage and remove and discard the central stalk. Shred the cabbage finely, cover with salt and leave for 24 hours. Drain through a colander and wipe carefully with kitchen paper or a soft clean cloth. Place into sterilised jars and cover with the pickling vinegar. Seal and leave to mature for a week or so. The longer you leave before eating, the softer the cabbage will become.

FOR PICKLED ONIONS

500g small pickling onions
1 tsp coriander seeds
about 500ml pickling vinegar

To remove their skins, immerse the onions in boiling water for 30 seconds, then drain them. The skins should peel away very easily. Dry the peeled onions thoroughly and cover with salt for 24 hours. Drain and wipe away any excess salt. Divide into sterilised pickling jars and add ½ teaspoon of coriander seeds to each jar before pouring over the vinegar. Seal and store for a week before eating.

FOR PICKLED BEETROOT

1kg beetroots
about 500ml pickling vinegar

Trim the stalks and bottom roots 5mm away from the beets, taking care not to cut the skin. Place in a pan of boiling water and simmer gently for 1 hour. Drain away the hot water and replace with cold. Once cool enough to handle, remove the remaining stalk and root and peel the beets. Cut into wedges and divide between sterilised pickling jars. Cover with the vinegar and seal. Leave to mature for a week or more.

Pickles will keep for up to a year unopened. Once opened, keep refrigerated.

A Salad Fit For a King

SERVES A VERY ROYAL 4

This really is a salad fit for a king. It's the combination of 'lashings of hard-boiled eggs' and the liberal scattering of mustard and cress leaves that crown this dish.

1 green lettuce
4 large tomatoes
1 small onion
1 bunch radishes
2 carrots
mustard and cress
4 hard-boiled eggs

TO SERVE
Home-made Salad Cream (see page 48), or olive oil and ½ lemon

Remove the stalk from the lettuce and shred into a large salad bowl. Slice the tomatoes and add to the bowl. Peel and slice the onion very thinly into rings and add these to the salad. Top and tail the radishes, then halve lengthways and add to the bowl. Peel the carrots and grate them into the bowl. Add a liberal scattering of fresh mustard and cress and turn gently with salad servers. Peel the eggs and cut into quarters lengthways, then arrange them over the top of the salad.

Serve with spoonfuls of home-made salad cream or, if you prefer, dress with olive oil and a squeeze of fresh lemon juice.

'The high tea that awaited them was truly magnificent. A huge ham gleaming as pink as Timmy's tongue; a salad fit for a king. In fact, as Dick said, fit for several kings, it was so enormous. It had in it everything that anyone could possibly want. "Lettuce, tomatoes, onions, radishes, mustard and cress, carrot grated up – this is carrot, isn't it, Mrs Penruthlan?" said Dick. "And lashings of hard-boiled eggs."'

(FIVE GO DOWN TO THE SEA)

Scotch Eggs

MAKES 4

Scotch eggs are the perfect picnic food, keeping fresh and whole in their own little jackets of breadcrumby goodness.

5 free-range eggs
500g free-range pork mince
2 fresh sage leaves
1 small onion
salt and freshly ground black pepper
2 thick bread slices
vegetable oil, for frying

Place 4 of the eggs in a saucepan, cover with water and bring to the boil. Boil for 3½–5 minutes, then remove from pan and leave to stand in cold water until cool. Peel the eggs carefully.

Place the pork mince in a bowl. Finely chop the sage leaves and add to the bowl. Grate in the onion. Add a pinch of salt and a good grind of black pepper. Mix thoroughly with your hands. Divide the mixture into four equal portions, roll into balls and flatten them out onto a lightly floured surface. Wrap the boiled eggs in the meat patties and form into large balls. Place on a plate and refrigerate for 30 minutes.

Beat the remaining uncooked egg and use it to coat the Scotch eggs. Blitz the bread slices to breadcrumbs and spread out on a clean plate. Roll the coated Scotch eggs in the breadcrumbs to cover them all over.

Heat 2cm of oil in a small frying pan or wok and fry the Scotch eggs one by one until the breadcrumbs are a deep golden brown. Soft-centred eggs are best eaten warm, while the hard-boiled variety will keep in a fridge for a couple of days.

Coleslaw

SERVES 4

A jolly fine coleslaw is a real treat on a picnic, and the key to this champion of salads is to slice the cabbage and onion as fine as you can possibly get them.

1 small white cabbage
1 medium onion
2 large carrots
1 apple
2 tbsp mayonnaise
1 tbsp plain yoghurt
handful of raisins
45g sunflower seeds
salt and freshly ground black pepper

Chop the cabbage in half lengthways and cut out and discard the tough 'core' at the base. Slice the cabbage as finely as you can and place in a large bowl. Finely slice the onion and add to the bowl. Peel the carrots and grate them into the bowl. Halve the apple, discard the core and chop into 5mm chunks, then add to the bowl.

Add the mayonnaise, plain yoghurt, raisins and sunflower seeds and give it all a good stir, making sure the mayonnaise and yoghurt are evenly distributed. Season well with salt and black pepper to taste.

Allowing the coleslaw to stand in the fridge for half an hour before serving will give the flavours a chance to develop.

Drop Scones

MAKES 10

"“Look at that cream cheese, too,” marvelled Dick, quite overcome. “And that fruit cake. And are those drop-scones, or what? Are we supposed to have something of everything, Mrs Penruthlan?”'
(FIVE GO DOWN TO THE SEA)

Also known as Scotch pancakes, these delightful little treats are great devoured in copious quantities for breakfast with golden syrup and thick cream, or spread thinly with jam on a picnic.

125g plain flour
1 tsp baking powder
25g caster sugar
25g butter
2 eggs
pinch salt
100ml milk
sunflower oil, for frying

Sift the flour into a bowl together with the baking powder and sugar. Add the butter, crack in the eggs and mix with a wooden spoon. Add the salt and a little of the milk to loosen the mixture. Beat well, adding the rest of the milk a little at a time until you have a smooth batter with the consistency of thick cream.

Warm a little oil in a heavy-based pan and drop in a ladleful of batter. Cook for 2–3 minutes and then flip with a spatula and cook the other side until it too is golden brown. Repeat to use up all the batter, adding extra oil to the pan if necessary.

'A voice came up the stairs. "Come down to tea, children, because there are hot scones for you, just out of the oven."'
(FIVE ON KIRRIN ISLAND AGAIN)

Aunt Fanny's Best Scones

MAKES ABOUT 12

Are you a 'scons' or a 'scoans' person? The Five would never have wasted time arguing over how to pronounce it, they'd have tucked straight in with a polite thank-you to Aunt Fanny, or whoever had just made them. No doubt the scones would be covered with a healthy amount of strawberry jam and clotted cream too.

450g self-raising flour
2 tsp baking powder
100g butter, plus extra for greasing
50g caster sugar
2 free-range eggs
a little milk

TO SERVE
Strawberry Jam (see page 25)
clotted cream

YOU WILL NEED
scone cutter

Preheat the oven to 200°C/fan 180°C/400°F/gas 6, and grease and line a baking sheet with parchment paper.

Sift the flour and baking powder into a large bowl and rub in the butter until you have a breadcrumb consistency. Add the sugar and work through with your fingers. Crack in the eggs and stir in a drop of milk, enough to form a soft dough.

Tip onto a lightly floured surface and knead gently, then roll out to a thickness of 2cm. Cut with a scone cutter and place on the baking sheet. Bake in the oven for 10–15 minutes until the scones have risen and turned a golden brown. Remove to cool on a cooling rack and serve with liberal amounts of jam and cream.

Ginger Biscuits

MAKES UP TO 20

'"What shall we do this afternoon?" said Dick, when they had finished munching the delicious ginger biscuits. "I say, aren't these good? You know, I do think good cooks deserve some kind of decoration, just as much as good soldiers or scientists, or writers. I should give Joanna the OBCBE."
"Whatever's that?" said Julian.
"Order of the Best Cooks of the British Empire," said Dick grinning.'
(FIVE ON KIRRIN ISLAND AGAIN)

The Famous Five loved all things which contained ginger. Ginger is one of the oldest spices known; originally cultivated in the Far East, it was eaten by Chinese sailors to ward off scurvy. Its use in Europe dates back to the first century CE and it was a highly popular ingredient in Elizabethan times.

125g unsalted butter
100g dark muscovado sugar
4 tbsp golden syrup
325g plain flour
1 tsp bicarbonate of soda
2 tsp ground ginger

Preheat the oven to 170°C/fan 150°C/325°F/gas 3 and grease a baking sheet.

Melt the butter, sugar and syrup in a saucepan over a low heat.

Sift the flour, bicarbonate of soda and ground ginger into a large bowl and stir in the melted ingredients to make a stiff dough. Roll out on a lightly floured surface to a thickness of about 5mm. Using a pastry cutter, cut to shape and transfer to the baking sheet. Bake in the oven for 10 minutes or until the biscuits are golden brown.

Lemon Biscuits

MAKES ABOUT 25

'"Anyone hungry?" asked Anne. "I could do with some cake and biscuits."'
(FIVE ON A HIKE TOGETHER)

Biscuits, yummy biscuits. Watch out, Timmy will have all those if he gets a sniff.

250g butter
140g caster sugar
zest of 2 lemons
1 egg yolk
2 tsp vanilla extract
300g plain flour

Preheat the oven to 180°C/fan 160°C/350°F/gas 4 and line a baking sheet with parchment paper.

Beat the butter and sugar together in a mixing bowl using a wooden spoon. Add the lemon zest, egg yolk and vanilla extract and beat some more.

Sift in the flour and beat in with the spoon. When thoroughly mixed, chill in the fridge for 30 minutes. Roll out onto greaseproof paper and cut to the desired shape using a biscuit cutter. The size cutter you use will determine the number of biscuits in the tin! Place on the baking sheet and bake in the oven for 12–15 minutes or until a pale golden colour. These biscuits are best left to cool on a rack before eating.

Jam Tarts

MAKES 12

It wasn't the knave of hearts who stole the tarts, it was Julian in his daring raid on the larder during the terrible Mrs Stick's tenure as cook at Kirrin Cottage. Mean old Mrs Stick, a temporary cook, taken on at Kirrin Cottage by Aunt Fanny, refused to feed the children in the style to which they'd become accustomed. Jam tarts make a frequent appearance throughout the books, but Julian only has to resort to sneakiness in *Five Run Away Together*.

225g plain flour
110g butter
80g caster sugar
1 egg
a little milk
12 heaped tsp Strawberry Jam (see page 25)

YOU WILL NEED
12-cup tart tray

Preheat the oven to 180°C/fan 160°C/350°F/gas 4 and grease a 12-cup tart tray.

Sift the flour into a bowl and rub in the butter until you have the consistency of breadcrumbs. Add the sugar and mix through with your fingers. Mix in the egg and a splash of milk to form a thick dough.

Roll out the dough to a thickness of 5mm on a floured surface. Using a medium pastry cutter, cut the dough into 12 circles and place them in the tart tray. Add a heaped teaspoon of jam to each tart and bake in the oven for 10 minutes until the pastry is a light golden brown.

'He felt along the shelf again and came to a plate on which were what he thought must be jam-tarts, for they were round and flat, and had something sticky in the middle.'
(FIVE RUN AWAY TOGETHER)

'"I'll get you some supper," said Anne to everyone. "We're all famished."'
(FIVE GO OFF IN A CARAVAN)

Chapter Three

SCRUMPTIOUS SUPPERS

Aunt Fanny's Tomato Soup

SERVES 4

"'Oh, I'm terribly hungry," said Dick. He sniffed, holding his nose up in the air just as Timmy often did. "I believe you've been making your special tomato soup, with real tomatoes, Aunt Fanny!"'
(FIVE HAVE PLENTY OF FUN)

Aunt Fanny may not have been able to lay her hands on a couple of red peppers, but they certainly make a worthwhile tasty addition to this modern take on the Famous Five's favourite soup.

2 red peppers
8 tomatoes
1 litre boiling water
2 tbsp olive oil
1 white onion
1 garlic clove
1 tbsp plain flour
2 tsp paprika
1 tsp bouillon or 1 vegetable stock cube
500ml cold water
salt and freshly ground black pepper

Chargrill the peppers by placing them under the grill or holding them directly over a gas flame using tongs. Turn them regularly until they become blackened on all sides. This will take 5 minutes or so. When done, place the peppers in a zip-lock plastic food bag and allow to cool (this will make it easier to remove the blackened skins).

To peel the tomatoes, first cut a small 'x' on the bottom of each one, then place them in a bowl and cover with the boiling water. Allow to stand for a few minutes until the skins begin to peel away. Remove the skins, starting at the 'x' you made on each base and discard, but be sure to keep the tomato water. Chop the tomatoes and set aside.

TO SERVE (OPTIONAL)
1 tbsp chopped fresh chives
small pot double cream

YOU WILL NEED
zip-lock plastic food bag

Heat the oil in a saucepan and chop the onion and garlic. Add the onion to the pan and simmer until it begins to turn translucent and then add the garlic. Simmer gently until the onion turns a lovely golden colour. Add the flour, paprika, bouillon and a good pinch of salt to the onion and garlic and stir well. Cook for a couple of minutes, stirring continuously to prevent it sticking on the bottom of the pan. Next, add the chopped tomatoes to the pan together with some of the reserved tomato water, stir and turn down to the lowest heat.

Remove the peppers from the plastic bag and, using a knife, scrape off the charred black skin. Halve the peppers, and remove and discard the seeds. Roughly chop the peppers and add them to the saucepan together with the rest of the tomato water and the additional 500ml water. Place a lid on the pan, turn up the heat and bring to the boil, then reduce the heat and simmer very gently for 30 minutes. Remove the soup from the heat and pour into a blender. Blitz until smooth and season to taste.

Serve in bowls topped with a few chopped chives and a swirl of cream if you like.

"“My word!” said Julian, admiringly. “You do know how to stock a larder, I must say, Mrs Stick. A roast chicken! I thought I smelt one cooking.”'
(FIVE RUN AWAY TOGETHER)

Roast Chicken

SERVES 4

During the rationing years, a chicken was more valuable kept alive as a source of eggs, rather than served up roasted on a Sunday afternoon. The Five did eat a roast chicken, though, and rather surprisingly it was the stingy cook Mrs Stick who provided it.

1 medium-sized free-range chicken
1 lemon
a few fresh thyme sprigs
butter
sea salt and freshly ground black pepper

Preheat the oven to 200°C/fan 180°C/350°F/gas 6.

Place the chicken in a roasting tin and make snips in the skin over both breasts and on the drumsticks. Carefully peel the zest from the lemon and snip into 1cm pieces. Strip the leaves from the thyme (reserve a sprig for the cavity) and discard the stalks. Take a pinch of butter and combine with a few thyme leaves and a piece of lemon zest. Do this several times and tuck into the slits in the chicken skin.

Halve the zested lemon and tuck inside the body cavity with a sprig of thyme and a knob of butter. Season the bird liberally with sea salt and black pepper.

Place in the hot oven. Remove the bird after 1 hour and baste it with the juices in the bottom of the roasting tin. Roast for another 30 minutes until the chicken is cooked through. A medium chicken will normally cook in 1½ hours, but be sure to ask your butcher or check the packaging for cooking times.

Chicken Soup

SERVES 4

'They were just in time for their dinner. Block was there to serve it, and so was Sarah. The children sat down hungrily, in spite of having had coffee and buns. Block and Sarah ladled out hot soup on to their plates.'
(FIVE GO TO SMUGGLER'S TOP)

Soup was an excellent way of making the most of the ration back in the 1950s. Today it is still a great way to make use of any leftovers. Chicken soup is the perfect follow-up to a Sunday roast. Unless, of course, like the Five you've managed to devour every scrap of meat on the carcass. In which case you'll need a fresh one.

FOR THE CHICKEN AND STOCK

- *1 small free-range chicken*
- *1 onion*
- *1 leek*
- *1 carrot*
- *2 celery sticks*
- *1 tsp whole black peppercorns*
- *pinch salt*

Place the chicken in a large stockpot. Halve the onion, leaving the skin on. Chop the leek, carrot and celery into 2cm chunks. Add the vegetables to the stockpot, together with the peppercorns and salt. Add enough water to cover the chicken and bring to the boil. Turn down the heat, place a lid on the pot and simmer for 1 hour. Remove the chicken from the pot and allow to cool. Strain the stock through a colander and keep 1l of the liquid. Discard the skin and remove all the meat from the chicken, then cut it into bite-size pieces, ready to add to the soup.

To make the soup, peel and chop the carrot into 5mm dice and thinly slice the leek. Halve the fennel bulb lengthways,

FOR THE SOUP

1 carrot
1 leek
1 fennel bulb
knob of butter
2 tsp plain flour
250ml double cream
salt and freshly ground black pepper
crusty bread, to serve

then turn onto the cut side and slice very thinly at 90 degrees. Melt the butter in a large saucepan, add the chopped vegetables and simmer gently for 5 minutes. Add the flour and stir well. Next, add the chicken meat and stir in the reserved stock a little at a time. Bring to the boil then turn down the heat and simmer gently for 20 minutes until the soup begins to thicken a little. Stir in the cream and simmer very gently for a further 5 minutes. Season to taste and serve with hunks of crusty bread.

Sausage & Mash & Onion Gravy

SERVES 4

'The policeman had seen them from his window and he came out, wiping his mouth. He wasn't very pleased at having to come out in the middle of a nice meal of sausage and onions.'
(FIVE ON A HIKE TOGETHER)

All of that hiking, cycling, gallivanting and rowing out to Kirrin Island was fuelled by a healthy intake of good home-made fresh food. The Famous Five, though, might have wanted to have a little lie down after this hearty dish of sausage and mash.

1kg King Edward potatoes
50ml double cream or milk
2 large knobs of butter
salt and freshly ground black pepper
8 fat pork sausages
1 large white onion
1 tbsp plain flour
pinch mixed herbs
1 beef stock cube
500ml potato water
vegetable oil, for frying

Peel and quarter the potatoes, place them in a large saucepan with a litre of salted water and boil until soft. Drain the potatoes, reserving 500ml of the cooking water in a measuring jug. Return the potatoes to the pan with the cream or milk and add a large knob of butter, a pinch of salt and a hearty grind of black pepper. Cover and leave to sit off the heat.

While the potatoes are cooking, fry the sausages for 10 minutes or so in a deep-sided frying pan. Turn them regularly to ensure the skin is a lovely brown all over.

To make the gravy, remove the cooked sausages from the pan and place them in a low oven to keep warm. Peel and chop the onion. Add the remaining knob of butter to the pan and fry the onion until it begins to turn golden brown. Add the flour and stir well. Continue to cook for a minute or so longer then add the mixed herbs and stock cube, and stir in a little of the reserved potato water. Continue adding the water, stirring well as you do so. Simmer the gravy until it begins to thicken.

Returning to the potatoes, remove the lid from the pan and mash thoroughly. Spoon onto warm plates, top with two sausages each and serve covered in the onion gravy.

'There was an enormous tureen of new potatoes, all gleaming with melted butter, scattered with parsley.'
(FIVE GO DOWN TO THE SEA)

New Potatoes with Melted Butter & Parsley

SERVES 4

A bowl of delicious baby new potatoes, running with butter and scattered with chopped parsley, is a meal in its own right. When in season, Jersey Royals really take some beating.

500g baby new potatoes
pinch salt
large knob of butter
handful of chopped flat-leaf parsley

Place the potatoes in a large saucepan and cover with cold water, add the salt and bring to the boil. Cook for about 10 minutes, or until the potatoes are tender.

Drain well and place in a small bowl, or a tureen as the Five would call it. Add the butter and chopped parsley. Stir through with a spoon, making sure that every potato is coated with melting butter.

A Famous Christmas Dinner

SERVES 4

'Joanna the cook was busy baking Christmas cakes. An enormous turkey had been sent over from Kirrin Farm, and was hanging up in the larder. Timothy thought it smelt glorious, and Joanna was always shooing him out of the kitchen.'
(FIVE GO ADVENTURING AGAIN)

Turkeys first made an appearance in Britain in the early part of the sixteenth century. They soon became popular and replaced goose as a Christmas meal as they were much cheaper and easier to raise, although they remained a luxury meat until the late 1950s when they became more affordable.

1 turkey crown
6 slices smoked streaky bacon
olive oil
salt and freshly ground black pepper
a few floury potatoes
1 garlic bulb

FOR THE CRANBERRY SAUCE
450g fresh cranberries
100g sugar
100ml orange juice
1 cinnamon stick

Preheat the oven to 180°C/fan 160°C/350°F/gas 4.

First, make the cranberry sauce. Combine all of the ingredients in a saucepan and bring to the boil, then turn the heat down to a gentle simmer for 5 minutes. Remove from the heat and remove the cinnamon stick.

Cover the turkey crown with the slices of bacon. Rub with olive oil and sprinkle with salt and black pepper and place in a roasting tin. Peel and quarter the potatoes and arrange around the turkey. Separate out the individual garlic cloves and give them a bash with the flat blade of a knife. Scatter in the roasting dish among the potatoes.

TO SERVE
Tiny Boiled Carrots & Peas (see page 97)
roasted parsnips

Place the tin in the oven and roast for 1½ hours. Remove from the oven and turn over the potatoes. Baste the crown with a little of the juices from the roasting tin and return to the oven for a further 30 minutes. Cooking times will vary depending on the size of the crown – be sure to check the packaging for correct cooking times. Allow to rest for at least 20 minutes before carving. Serve with the potatoes and vegetables.

Veal & Ham Pie

SERVES 4

'"Home-made veal-and-ham-pie! Stuffed tomatoes! And what a salad – what's in it, Joanna? Radishes, cucumber, carrot, beetroot, hard-boiled eggs, tomatoes, peas – Joanna, you're a marvel! What is the pudding?" George asked.'
(FIVE ON A SECRET TRAIL)

Joanna was by far the favourite cook in the stories, and this pie was cooked up as part of a feast hard-earned after rounding up three crooks.

1 onion
1 ham hock
1 bouquet garni
1 tsp whole black peppercorns
1 celery stick
275g veal
2 hard-boiled eggs (see page 20)

FOR THE HOT WATER PASTRY CRUST
225g plain flour
pinch salt
1 egg
100ml water
75g lard
1 egg, beaten, for glazing

Chop the onion in half, skin on, and place in a large lidded saucepan together with the ham hock. Add the bouquet garni and peppercorns. Chop the celery and add to the pan. Cover well with water and bring to the boil. Turn down the heat and simmer with the lid on for 1½ hours. Top up with water if necessary. Remove the hock from the pan and allow to cool. Keep the strained stock.

While the ham is cooking, cut the veal into 1cm cubes and prepare the pastry crust. Combine the flour, salt and egg in a bowl. Bring the water and lard to the boil in a small saucepan. Once the lard has melted, pour the liquid into the bowl with the flour mixture. Mix to a dough using a wooden spoon and, as soon as it is cool enough to handle, roll into a ball and allow to rest for a few minutes. Wrap the dough in clingfilm and refrigerate for half an hour.

YOU WILL NEED
medium pie dish

Returning to the cooled ham hock, pick all of the meat, including any gelatinous bits, from the bone and roughly chop before combining with the diced veal.

Preheat the oven to 180°C/fan 160°C/350°F/gas 4.

Roll out three-quarters of the pastry on a lightly floured surface and use it to line a greased pie dish. Place a layer of meat in the bottom of the dish. Halve one of the hard-boiled eggs lengthways and place cut side down on the bottom layer of meat, then add another layer of meat over the top, followed by the other egg, also halved lengthways, then topped off with meat. Using the remaining pastry, form a lid and seal the pie. Make a small hole in the top of the pie and pour in the reserved stock until it overflows. Glaze the top with the beaten egg.

Cook in the oven for 1½ hours, until the pastry is golden and the filling is bubbling inside.

Fried Plaice & Chips

SERVES 2

Adventuring, as they often do, so close to the coast, it is surprising how little fish and seafood the Famous Five eat. The fish they do eat comes either in tins or in the form of anchovy paste. This delicious meal of home-made chips and fried plaice is one which Anne dreams of in *Five on a Secret Trail*.

vegetable oil, for deep-frying
2 large King Edward potatoes
2 thick slices white bread
1 egg
2 plaice fillets

Put a deep pan of oil onto a high heat and peel and chip the potatoes while the oil is heating up. Dry them thoroughly in a tea towel before placing very carefully into the hot oil using a slotted spoon. Remember, Joanna the cook might have said something like 'a good cook never fries, 'til they see the blue smoke rise', which was a handy phrase among home economists and is basically a means of making sure the oil is hot enough before deep-frying. Deep-fry the chips for about 15 minutes, or until they are golden brown. Remove with a slotted spoon to a bowl lined with kitchen paper to absorb any excess oil.

While the chips are frying, blitz the bread slices to breadcrumbs and spread them on a large plate. Beat the egg and coat the fish with it on both sides then dip the fillets in the breadcrumbs to coat evenly all over. Fry the fish in a little oil in a shallow frying pan, turning after 3 minutes to cook both sides. Serve with the chips.

Meat Pie

SERVES 4

'There was a large meat-pie with delicious-looking pastry on top, and a collection of buns, biscuits and oranges.'
(FIVE GET INTO TROUBLE)

As we know, the Famous Five were keen on pies, and the meat pie appears in several of the stories. This meat pie, complete with its own gravy, would definitely have been a favourite.

500g stewing steak
vegetable oil, for frying
1 medium white onion
1 tsp whole black peppercorns
1 tsp salt
1 beef stock cube
1 tsp mixed herbs
2 tsp plain flour
500ml water
200g puff pastry (see page 53) or ready-rolled sheet
1 egg yolk, beaten, for glazing

YOU WILL NEED
medium pie dish

If you're making the pastry, do this first (following the instructions on page 53).

Preheat the oven to 170°C/fan 150°C/325°F/gas 3.

Cut the steak into 1cm cubes. Warm a little oil in a deep-sided frying pan. Peel and chop the onion and add to the pan. Fry for 2–3 minutes then add the steak together with the peppercorns and salt. Crumble in the stock cube and add the mixed herbs and flour. Stir through and cook for a further minute.

Next, add the water a little at a time, stirring as you go. Bring to the boil, then turn down the heat to a low simmer for 10 minutes until the gravy begins to thicken. Transfer to a pie dish and top with a sheet of puff pastry, cutting away the excess and brushing with beaten egg to glaze. Make a small slit in the top to let the steam escape and place in the oven for 1 hour until the pastry is golden.

Pea & Ham Soup

SERVES 5

This soup isn't specifically mentioned in the stories, but the children consume large quantities of soup throughout the series and pea and ham is a great way to use up any leftover ham hocks – which appear in abundance at Kirrin Cottage.

FOR THE STOCK

1 onion
2 celery sticks
1 carrot
1 ham hock (roughly 1kg in weight)
6 whole black peppercorns
2 star anise

FOR THE SOUP

1 large onion
knob of butter
225g red split lentils or split peas
freshly ground black pepper

To make the stock, halve the onion, leaving the skin on, and chop the celery. Throw the onion and celery into a large stockpot with the carrot. Add the ham hock, peppercorns and star anise and cover with plenty of water. Bring to the boil then turn down the heat, cover with a lid, and simmer gently for 1 hour.

Remove from the heat and lift out the ham hock with a slotted spoon; set aside to cool. Sieve the stock into a jug for use later. Once the ham hock has cooled enough to handle, cut away the skin and discard. Next, strip the meat from the bone and roughly chop.

Peel and finely chop the onion for the soup and fry gently in the butter. Add the chopped meat from the hock. Throw in the lentils or split peas and stir well, seasoning with black pepper. Pour in 500ml of the reserved stock and 500ml water. Bring to the boil then turn down to a gentle simmer. After 20 minutes or so the soup will thicken as the lentils/peas cook through. Add a drop more water to loosen if necessary.

Chicken Stew

SERVES 4

'The supper was lovely. "What is in your pot?" asked Dick, accepting a second helping. "I've never tasted such a delicious stew in my life."'
(FIVE HAVE A WONDERFUL TIME)

The Five enjoy a chicken stew cooked over a fire while they are all off having a *Wonderful Time*. Mrs Alfredo, one of the circus people in the story, included hare and hedgehog in her stew, but paprika, chorizo and capsicum peppers make for more palatable alternatives here.

1 large onion
2 garlic cloves
100g chorizo
olive oil
4 chicken thighs
1 red pepper
1 yellow pepper
1 tsp paprika
1 tsp plain flour
1 small glass red wine
400g tin chopped tomatoes
1 litre vegetable stock
salt and freshly ground black pepper

Peel and chop the onion, garlic and the chorizo, with its skin removed. Warm a glug of olive oil in the bottom of a large stockpot over a medium heat and fry the onion until it starts to turn golden brown. Then add the garlic – adding it at this stage prevents it burning.

Next, add the chopped chorizo and the chicken thighs. Turn the chicken after 3–4 minutes using tongs so it browns all over. Cut the two peppers into thin slices and add to the pot along with the paprika and flour. Give it a quick stir and add the wine, chopped tomatoes and vegetable stock. Simmer gently, with a lid on, for 45 minutes, stirring occasionally, then season to taste.

This stew is great on its own, with huge hunks of crusty bread to mop up the juices.

Stuffed Tomatoes

SERVES 4

A somewhat exotic meal for our Famous feasters, here you'll find them stuffed with delicious rice and mushrooms.

250g basmati rice
6 whole black peppercorns
1 bay leaf
3 star anise
salt and freshly ground black pepper
1 tsp vegetable stock powder
500ml water
4 beef tomatoes
1 small onion
1 garlic clove
knob of butter
4 large flat mushrooms
olive oil

Preheat the oven to 180°C/fan 160°C/350°F/gas 4.

Place the rice, peppercorns, bay leaf, star anise, a pinch of salt and the stock powder into a large lidded saucepan and cover with the water. Bring to the boil, then immediately turn down the heat to low. Place a folded tea towel over the top of the pan and press the lid on, remembering to fold the edges of the towel onto the pan lid so they don't catch and burn. Leave to cook over the lowest heat for 10 minutes. Remove from the heat and leave to stand.

Cut the tops off the tomatoes (keep them for the 'lids') and scoop out the pulp. Save this to add to the stuffing mix below.

To prepare the stuffing, peel and finely chop the onion and garlic. Heat the butter in a frying pan and gently fry the onion and garlic. Throw in the pulp from the tomatoes. Next, chop the mushrooms into small pieces and add to the frying pan. Once the mushrooms have begun to absorb the butter and juices, add the cooked rice, season well and stir thoroughly so the mushrooms and onion are evenly distributed. Remove from heat.

Divide the rice into four, and fill each of the tomatoes. Place the tops back on the filled tomatoes. Finally, arrange the tomatoes into a shallow dish, drizzle with olive oil and bake in the oven for 20 minutes.

Poached Fish
with New Potatoes & Parsley Sauce

SERVES 2

When the Five get themselves *Into a Fix*, one of the meals they enjoy is 'boiled fish'. As fish was not rationed during the war, cod and haddock might both have been on the menu, but the risks of deep-sea fishing in times of conflict were so high that fresh fish was very scarce. It was certainly a real treat.

200g baby new potatoes
300g smoked haddock fillet
125ml milk
small pinch salt
freshly ground black pepper

FOR THE PARSLEY SAUCE
large knob of butter
1 tbsp plain flour
200ml whole milk
2 tbsp chopped curly-leaf parsley
salt and freshly ground black pepper

Put the potatoes on to boil in a small saucepan for 10 minutes or until cooked but firm.

Poach the fish for 10 minutes in the milk along with the salt and a few grinds of black pepper.

To make the parsley sauce, melt the butter in a saucepan and add the plain flour to make a dry paste. Cook for 2–3 minutes. Remove from the heat and add a little milk and stir to loosen the paste. Gradually add the rest of the milk, little by little, stirring with a wooden spoon to make sure no lumps appear. Return to the heat and bring to a simmer, stirring all the time. As the sauce begins to thicken add the parsley and season. Cook until the sauce coats the back of the wooden spoon then serve poured over the fish and potatoes.

Rabbit Stew

SERVES 4

'A rabbit lolloped near, its big ears standing straight up enquiringly. "Ah-the waiter!" said Julian at once. "What have you to offer us today bunny? A nice rabbit pie?"'
(FIVE GET INTO TROUBLE)

A rabbit stew presents a fine alternative to a pie.

- *1 carrot*
- *1 garlic clove*
- *1 large leek*
- *knob of butter*
- *1 rabbit (ask your butcher to joint it for you)*
- *1 tbsp plain flour*
- *10 baby new potatoes*
- *1 bouquet garni*
- *1.5 litres vegetable stock*
- *salt and freshly ground black pepper*

Preheat the oven to 170°C/fan 150°C/325°F/gas 3.

Peel and dice the carrot and chop the garlic very finely. Top and tail the leek and cut into thin slices.

Melt the butter in a flameproof casserole dish and add the vegetables. Stir well and fry gently for a couple of minutes.

Next, brown the rabbit joints in the casserole with the vegetables. Add the flour and cook for a further minute or so.

Halve the potatoes and add to the pot with the bouquet garni. Pour in the vegetable stock and stir well, making sure nothing is stuck to the bottom of the dish. Season well and place in the oven for 1 hour until everything is tender and the sauce has thickened.

"'Can't we help you to do something?" said Anne. "I've just seen all the peas you're going to shell. Piles of them!"
(FIVE GO DOWN TO THE SEA)

Tiny Boiled Carrots & Peas

SERVES 4

The Five seem to spend about as much time shelling peas as they do rambling around the countryside. This little duo of fresh vegetables would give them the ability to see in the dark on one of their many adventures.

1kg peas in their pods
500g Chantenay carrots
knob of butter
6–8 chopped fresh mint leaves

Shell the peas, and top and tail the carrots. Place the carrots in a pan of cold water, bring to the boil and cook for 5 minutes. Add the peas and cook for 2 minutes. Remove from the heat, drain well and pour into a tureen. Add the butter and chopped mint. Turn through with a spoon to make sure the vegetables are well coated.

'The children finished all the pie and the tarts, too.'
(FIVE RUN AWAY TOGETHER)

Chapter Four

CRACKING CAKES AND TASTY TREATS

Fruit Cake

SERVES 6

A fine fruit cake is the perfect thing to take with you when you're off on a picnic or going camping. It will keep well in a Tupperware box, and a slice or two will give you enough energy to push your camping cart up the steepest of hills.

114g butter, plus extra for greasing
114g sugar
2 eggs
170g plain flour
¼ tsp baking powder
60g currants
60g sultanas
30g preserved mixed peel

YOU WILL NEED
25cm square cake tin

Preheat the oven to 170°C/fan 150°C/325°F/gas 3, and grease and line a 25cm square cake tin with parchment paper.

Cream the butter and sugar together in a large bowl and beat in the eggs. Sift the flour and baking powder together in a separate bowl and fold into the batter. Add the fruit and peel and mix well.

Pour into the lined cake tin and bake in the oven for 1 hour. Make sure the cake is cooked through by stabbing it with a butter knife. If the knife comes out clean then the cake is ready. Otherwise replace in the oven for a few more minutes.

'"George, your mother makes the most heavenly fruit cake I ever tasted," said Dick to George, wishing Timmy would be quiet.'
(FIVE GO TO SMUGGLER'S TOP)

Milk Pudding

SERVES 4

Milk pudding, a nostalgic dish for many, is the perfect way to warm up after a winter's walk along the coast or through the countryside, as our young heroes were prone to doing.

butter, for greasing
2 tbsp cornflour
570ml whole milk
2 eggs
1 tbsp caster sugar
zest of ½ lemon
1 tsp ground cinnamon
handful of currants

YOU WILL NEED
medium pie dish

Preheat the oven to 170°C/fan 150°C/325°F/gas 3 and butter a medium pie dish.

Make a smooth paste with the cornflour and a little of the milk. Put the rest of the milk in a medium saucepan on the stove and bring to the boil. Once boiling, add the cornflour paste and stir continuously until the milk begins to thicken. Remove from the heat. Separate the eggs and beat the yolks. Add to the milk with the sugar and lemon zest and stir in well.

Beat the egg whites to a froth and fold them into the milk pan. Pour the mixture into the buttered pie dish, scatter over the ground cinnamon and currants and bake in the oven for 30 minutes until set.

Fresh Fruit Salad

SERVES 4

'"There it is on the sideboard," said Anne. "Wobbly blancmange, fresh fruit salad and jelly. I'm glad I'm hungry."'
(FIVE FALL INTO ADVENTURE)

Julian, Dick, George, Timmy and Anne always ate exceptionally well, so much so, in fact, that today's notion of getting our 'five a day' might well have been influenced by our intrepid explorers. Of course, all of the fruit in a fresh fruit salad back in the 1950s would have been seasonal.

2 oranges
150g seedless black grapes
6 Victoria plums
2 apples
100g raspberries
300ml orange juice
thick cream or evaporated milk, to serve

Peel the oranges, removing as much pith as possible from the fruit. Cut into 1cm pieces and place in a glass bowl. Remove the grapes from their stalks and slice in half lengthways. Place them in the bowl with the oranges.

Halve the plums and remove the stones, then core the apples. Cut the plums and apples into pieces about the same size as the oranges, and add them to the bowl along with the raspberries. Pour over the orange juice and allow to stand in the fridge for 10 minutes before serving, with thick cream or evaporated milk.

Plum Pie

SERVES 6

George's father, Uncle Quentin, could be a grumpy so-and-so at times, but this pie would surely have put a smile on his face had he showed up at the table.

FOR THE PASTRY
225g plain flour
100g butter
50g caster sugar
2 egg yolks
2 tbsp water

FOR THE PIE
400g ripe Victoria plums
750g caster sugar, plus 1 tsp to scatter
50ml orange juice
milk, for glazing
Vanilla Ice Cream (see page 122), to serve

YOU WILL NEED
shallow pie dish

Preheat the oven to 200°C/fan 180°C/400°F/gas 6.

To make the pastry, sift the flour into a bowl and rub in the butter. Add the sugar and mix through with your fingers. Add the egg yolks and the water and mix with a wooden spoon. Turn out onto a lightly floured surface and knead gently for a minute or two until smooth. Place in the fridge to rest for 30 minutes.

Wash, halve and de-stone the plums, then cut into quarters.

Reserve a third of the pastry and roll out the rest on a lightly floured surface. Use this to line a shallow pie dish. Layer the plum quarters into the pie and scatter each layer liberally with the sugar.

Pour in the orange juice and close the pie using the remaining pastry to form a lid. Crimp around the edges and make a small hole in the middle of the lid. Place in the oven. After 20 minutes, remove the pie, brush with milk and scatter a spoonful of sugar over the top.

Reduce the oven temperature to 170°C/fan 150°C/325°F/gas 3, replace the pie and bake for a further 20 minutes. Allow the pie to cool a little before serving with a scoop of luscious vanilla ice cream.

'George said nothing, but went on eating her plum-pie. She hadn't said a word all through the meal. Her father had not appeared at the table, much to the children's relief.'
(FIVE ON A TREASURE ISLAND)

Vanilla Custard

SERVES 6

'"Fried sausages and onions, potatoes, a tin of sliced peaches and I'll make a custard," said Anne, at once.'
(FIVE HAVE A WONDERFUL TIME)

With a host of sweet treats and puddings to help fuel your adventures, you'll be needing a big jug of vanilla custard to pour over the top before tucking in.

250ml milk
60ml whipping cream
3 egg yolks
75g caster sugar
2 tsp cornflour
1 tsp vanilla extract

Bring the milk and cream to the boil in a small saucepan and then remove from the heat immediately.

Beat the eggs and sugar in a bowl and whisk in the cornflour. Slowly add the cream and milk mixture, stirring continuously. Return the mixture to the saucepan and heat slowly to thicken. Stir in the vanilla extract and pour liberally over your pudding.

Ginger Cake

SERVES 4

'Aunt Fanny had baked new scones for them, and had made a ginger cake with black treacle. It was dark brown and sticky to eat. The children finished it all up and said it was the nicest they had ever tasted.'
(FIVE ON A TREASURE ISLAND)

Here is that ubiquitous ingredient, ginger, once more. This cake is a little lighter than the sticky ginger cake Aunt Fanny made as it uses golden syrup instead of treacle, but it definitely tastes just as nice.

200g golden caster sugar
150g butter, plus extra for greasing
200g golden syrup
400g plain flour
1 tsp ground cinnamon
2 tsp ground ginger
1 tsp bicarbonate of soda
50g chopped crystallised ginger
1 egg
250ml milk

YOU WILL NEED
20cm square cake tin

Preheat the oven to 170°C/fan 150°C/325°F/gas 3, and grease and line a 20cm square cake tin with parchment paper.

Melt the sugar, butter and syrup together in a saucepan. Sift the flour, cinnamon, ground ginger and bicarbonate of soda into a mixing bowl. Beat in the melted mixture together with the crystallised ginger, egg and milk. Mix well and tip into the cake tin. Bake in the oven for 1½ hours.

Christmas Cake

SERVES 8

Joanna the cook spends a deal of time preparing and making the Christmas cake at Kirrin Cottage, and here's a simple recipe based on an old one found in the 1949 edition of the Yorkshire Federation of Women's Institutes book of seven hundred recipes. The brandy is a later addition, and of course as the cake improves over a couple of weeks, you can always poke a few holes in it with a metal skewer and feed it once or twice with a little more brandy should you wish.

225g butter, plus extra for greasing
225g sugar
4 eggs
180g plain flour
60g ground almonds
125g sultanas
125g glacé cherries
225g currants
125g mixed peel
zest and juice of 1 lemon
½ tsp baking powder
2 tbsp brandy, plus extra to feed the cake (optional)

YOU WILL NEED
25 x 25 x 10cm cake tin

Preheat the oven to 170°C/fan 150°C/325°F/gas 3, and grease and line a 25 x 25 x 10cm cake tin with parchment paper.

Cream the butter and sugar together, then beat in the eggs. Stir in the flour and ground almonds, add the fruit and the lemon zest and juice. Stir in the baking powder and brandy and leave to stand for a few minutes. Pour the cake mixture into the prepared cake tin. Next, line the *outside* of the cake tin with newspaper tied with string as this will help prevent the cake burning at the edges. Bake in the oven for 4 hours.

'It really was a jolly Christmas Day. There were no lessons, of course, and there were to be none the next day either. The children gave themselves up to the enjoyment of eating a great deal, sucking sweets, and looking forward to the lighting of the Christmas tree.'

(FIVE GO ADVENTURING AGAIN)

Treacle Tart

SERVES 4

The sweetest of all puddings, a treacle tart is the perfect end to a hearty meal. A dollop of vanilla ice cream and a coating of fresh cream make for a simply wizard match.

FOR THE SHORT-CRUST PASTRY BASE

225g plain flour
110 butter
1 egg

FOR THE FILLING

4 slices soft white bread, crusts removed
4 tbsp golden syrup
½ tsp mixed spice

TO SERVE

Vanilla Ice Cream (see page 122)
single cream

Preheat the oven to 190°C/fan 170°C/375°F/gas 5.

First, make the pastry. Sift the flour into a mixing bowl and rub in the butter. Beat the egg and add it to the bowl. Combine to form a dough. Roll out the dough on a floured surface and use it to line a greased flan dish. Prick the bottom well with a fork and leave in the fridge for 30 minutes. Line the pastry with parchment paper and weigh it down with dried peas or baking beads. Blind bake the pastry case in the oven for 10–15 minutes until pale golden.

To make the filling, blitz the bread slices to breadcrumbs and mix them in a bowl with the golden syrup and mixed spice. When the pastry case is ready, fill with the mixture.

Reduce the oven temperature to 180°C/fan 160°C/350°F/gas 4 and bake for 20 minutes until the pastry is a lovely darker golden colour. Transfer to a wire rack to cool a little before serving with cream or ice cream.

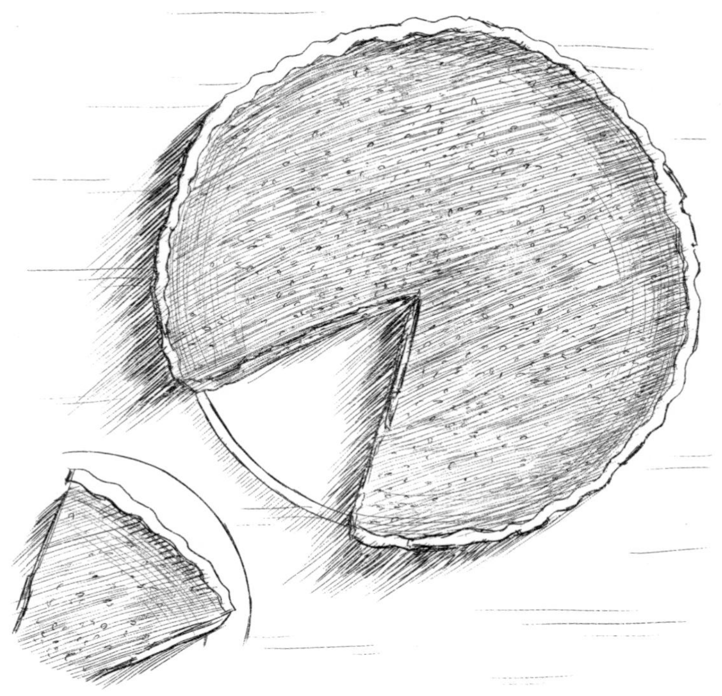

'With two or three great gulps Timmy cleared his plate, and then sat waiting for any scraps of treacle tart that might descend his way.'
(FIVE RUN AWAY TOGETHER)

Mint Humbugs

MAKES ABOUT 20

Few home chefs these days heat sugar to 126°C and then attempt to shape it with their own two hands, but it's worth a go if you have a free Sunday afternoon! These sweets make a great gift.

450g caster sugar
170ml water
1 tsp peppermint essence
1 tsp cream of tartar
green food colouring
icing sugar, for dusting

YOU WILL NEED
cooking thermometer
2 silicone baking mats

Place the sugar and water in a large saucepan and heat slowly until all the sugar has dissolved. Add the peppermint essence and cream of tartar and bring to a rolling boil for 8 minutes or until the liquid reaches a temperature of 126°C on a cooking thermometer. Pour half onto a silicone baking mat and set aside. Add a few drops of food colouring to the pan to colour the remaining mixture and stir. Once the colour has dispersed evenly, pour onto a separate silicone baking mat.

Working with the undyed mixture first, roll it in the mat to form a 'snake' and stretch out from end to end to a length of about 20cm. Do the same with the coloured mixture. Place the green snake on top of the white one and twist either end in opposite directions to make a twist. Using kitchen scissors or a sharp knife, cut the humbugs into 1cm pieces and allow to cool completely. Dust with icing sugar and store in a tin. The humbugs will keep for up to six months in a tin.

Toffee

MAKES ABOUT 1kg

The Famous Five were very sparing when it came to scoffing toffees, perhaps because free dental care was some way off when they were all young. But if you're doing as much exercise as them and eating a similar balanced diet, you can afford to treat yourself with a few of these delicious sweets.

900g sugar
110g unsalted butter, plus extra for greasing
250ml whole milk
397g tin condensed milk
drop of vanilla extract

Liberally grease a 44 x 29cm shallow baking tray.

Warm the sugar, butter and milk in a large saucepan, stirring with a wooden spoon. Slowly add the condensed milk and bring to the boil once all the sugar has dissolved. Boil steadily for 20 minutes.

Remove from the heat and stir in the vanilla extract. Bring to the boil once more for a further 5 minutes, then pour into the prepared baking tray and allow to cool before breaking into pieces. Not that they will last that long, but these toffees will keep in a tin for weeks.

'They enjoyed their walk. They went into a quaint old coffee shop and had steaming cups of delicious creamy coffee and jammy buns. Timmy had two of the buns and gobbled them greedily.'
(FIVE GO TO SMUGGLER'S TOP)

Jammy Buns

MAKES 16

If you're lucky, you might find a 'quaint old coffee shop' that will serve up steaming hot cups of delicious creamy coffee and these jammy buns. If not, then they are just as wonderful made yourself. The recipe uses margarine, which was invented in France towards the end of the nineteenth century and, by the 1950s, had found its way into shops as a cheaper alternative to butter. It is, of course, ideal for cake making on account of its softness.

225g self-raising flour
pinch salt
80g margarine, plus extra for greasing
80g caster sugar
2 eggs
raspberry or strawberry jam (about 8 tsp)

Preheat the oven to 200°C/fan 180°C/400°F/gas 6 and grease a couple of baking trays.

Sift the flour and salt into a bowl and rub in the margarine until you have the texture of breadcrumbs. Next, add the sugar and work through with your fingers. Crack in the eggs and mix with a wooden spoon to form a dough.

Divide the dough into 16 even pieces and form them into balls. Place them on the greased baking trays spaced apart. Make a hole in each of the balls and spoon a little jam inside, then close the hole over. Bake in the oven for 20 minutes. Allow to cool before eating – that jam will be hot!

Ginger Buns

MAKES ABOUT 12

'"I think her ginger buns are gorgeous," said Anne. "Especially when they are all hot from the oven."'
(FIVE GO TO SMUGGLER'S TOP)

Since it first arrived on these shores with the Romans, ginger has long been revered for its medicinal properties. It was even thought to ward off the plague. For the Famous Five who devoured it in various forms – biscuits, bread, beer, cake and buns – it helped ward off villains, ruffians, smugglers and spies.

135g butter
170g sugar
2 eggs
1 tsp ground ginger
225g plain flour
2 tsp baking powder

YOU WILL NEED
cupcake tin

Preheat the oven to 180°C/fan 160°C/350°F/gas 4 and line a cupcake tin with cases.

Cream the butter, sugar, eggs and ground ginger together in a bowl. In a separate bowl, sift the flour and baking powder together, then fold into the batter. Mix well and spoon into the bun cases. Place in the oven and bake for 20 minutes until golden.

Shortbread

MAKES 20 FINGERS

'"I shall look after the food side for you," said Anne. "But George must help with the preparing of the meals and washing-up. See, George?" George didn't see. She hated doing all the things that girls had to do, such as making beds and washing-up. She looked sulky.'
(FIVE GO OFF TO CAMP)

The Famous Five stories are very much of their time, and one of the things that marks this is the fact that it is always Anne who takes on the job of preparing meals and then clearing up, unlike today. The boys and Georgina seldom lift a finger to help out, unless, of course, it's a shortbread finger!

225g softened butter, plus extra for greasing
115g caster sugar, plus extra to sprinkle
340g plain flour

Preheat the oven to 150°C/fan 130°C/300°F/gas 2, and grease and line two medium-sized 2cm deep baking trays with parchment paper.

Beat the butter and sugar together in a large bowl. Fold in the flour and mix well to form a dough. Divide the dough in half and spread out evenly in the lined baking trays, to a thickness of 2 cm. Prick the surface of the dough all over with a fork and place in the oven for 40 minutes until the biscuits turn the colour of straw.

Remove from the oven, coat the tops with plenty of caster sugar and cut to fingers in the tins while still warm. Place on a wire rack to cool a little.

Chocolate Cake

SERVES 8

It's clear that all four children are aware of the value of eating a balanced diet. All of the stories mention sweets and treats of some sort, and chocolate cake is devoured once the Five are *on Kirrin Island Again*, but these treats are never eaten to excess, even if they do on occasion have cake for breakfast!

FOR THE SPONGE
170g self-raising flour
170g caster sugar
170g margarine, plus extra for greasing
3 eggs
1 tbsp cocoa powder
1 tsp baking powder

FOR THE BUTTERCREAM FILLING
100g icing sugar
50g softened butter
1 tbsp cocoa powder

YOU WILL NEED
2 round cake tins

Preheat the oven to 180°C/fan 160°C/350°F/gas 4, and grease and line two round cake tins with parchment paper.

Beat all the sponge ingredients together in a mixing bowl. Add more cocoa powder if you want a darker chocolate cake. Divide the cake batter evenly between the two greased cake tins and bake in the oven for 25 minutes, until a butter knife inserted into the centre of the cake comes out clean.

Prepare the filling by combining the icing sugar, butter and cocoa powder and beating until smooth. Spread liberally between the two chocolate cake halves and sandwich the sponges together. This will keep in a cake tin for a couple of days.

'George went to hunt in the larder for the tea-things. There was certainly plenty of food! She cut some bread and butter, found some new honey, brought out a huge chocolate cake and some ginger buns, and put the kettle on to boil.'
(FIVE ON KIRRIN ISLAND AGAIN)

Apple Pie

SERVES 6

"'Hm! Salad. Hard-boiled eggs. Slices of ham. And what's this – apple-pie! My goodness! Don't tell me you cooked that here, Anne.'"
(FIVE GO OFF TO CAMP)

A generous slice of apple pie all covered in thick cream, what's not to like?

225g plain flour
100g butter
150g caster sugar
2 egg yolks
2 tbsp water
450g Bramley apples
milk, for glazing
double cream, to serve

YOU WILL NEED
shallow pie dish

Preheat the oven to 200°C/fan 180°C/400°F/gas 6.

For the pastry, sift the flour into a bowl and rub in the butter. Add 100g of the sugar and mix through with your fingers. Add the egg yolks and the water and mix with a wooden spoon. Turn out onto a lightly floured surface and knead gently for a minute or two until smooth. Place in the fridge to rest for 30 minutes.

Reserve a third of the pastry and roll out the rest on a lightly floured surface. Use this to line a shallow pie dish. Peel and core the apples and slice thinly into the pie. Scatter liberally with the rest of the sugar (though you don't have to use all of it).

Add 50ml of water and close the pie using the remaining pastry to form a lid. Seal the edges and make a small hole in the middle of the lid.

Place in the oven. After 20 minutes, remove the pie and brush with milk. Reduce the oven temperature to 170°C/fan 150°C/325°F/gas 3, replace the pie and bake for a further 20 minutes. Allow the pie to cool a little before serving with double cream.

Vanilla Ice Cream

MAKES 1 × 600ml TUPPERWARE CONTAINER

'The tinkle of an ice-cream man's bell was heard in the distance. Julian felt in his pocket. He jumped up and rushed off, jingling his money.'
(FIVE ON A TREASURE ISLAND)

Ices are very popular with the children and make an appearance in seven of the stories. Vanilla is an all-time classic and really easy to make at home.

2 vanilla pods
500ml double cream
70g sugar
3 egg yolks

Halve the vanilla pods lengthways and scrape away the seeds. Heat the cream slowly in a saucepan with the vanilla pods. As it comes to the boil, add the sugar and stir until thoroughly dissolved. Remove from the heat.

Whisk the egg yolks separately in a bowl. Add them to the warm cream and sugar. Pass through a sieve into a clean Tupperware container, allow to cool completely then freeze. This will keep well in the freezer for up to 6 months.

Sticky Gingerbread

MAKES 8 THICK SLICES

'There were home-made scones with new honey. There were slices of bread thickly spread with butter, and new-made cream cheese to go with it. There was sticky brown gingerbread, hot from the oven, and a big solid fruit cake that looked almost like a plum pudding when it was cut, it was so black.'
(FIVE GO OFF TO CAMP)

This super-sticky gingerbread may take a while to bake, but only minutes to devour.

225g butter, plus extra for greasing
225g soft brown sugar
225g black treacle
225g plain flour
2 eggs
2 tbsp ground ginger
1 tbsp ground cinnamon
1 tsp bicarbonate of soda
50ml warm milk

YOU WILL NEED
25cm cake tin

Preheat the oven to 170°C/fan 150°C/325°F/gas 3 and liberally grease a 25cm square cake tin.

Cream the butter and sugar in a bowl, then add the treacle. Sift in the flour, and add the eggs and spices. Dissolve the bicarbonate of soda in the warm milk and add to the bowl. Mix well with a wooden spoon. Bake in the greased cake tin for 2 hours. Allow to cool before turning out and cutting into slices.

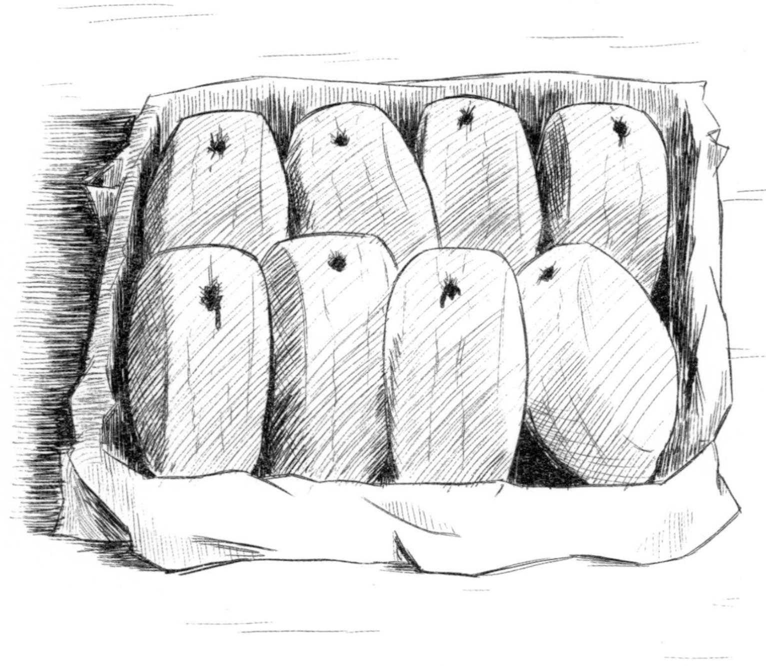

Doughnuts

MAKES 12

'They took Timmy by the collar, and went out through the turnstiles, click-click-click. "I feel like having a couple of doughnuts at the dairy," said George. "And some lemonade. Anyone else feel the same?"'
(FIVE HAVE A WONDERFUL TIME)

Doughnuts are a favourite at fairgrounds and country shows, but Julian, Dick, George and Anne get theirs from the dairy in a village nearby to where they are staying in their caravans.

500g plain flour
1 tsp baking powder
75g butter
75g sugar
250ml milk
1 egg
sunflower oil, for frying
caster sugar for coating

YOU WILL NEED
2 biscuit cutters, 1 half the size of the other

Sift the flour and baking powder together in a mixing bowl. Rub in the butter, then add the sugar and work through with your fingers. Add the milk and egg and beat the mixture to form a soft dough. Refrigerate for 30 minutes.

Pour about 1cm of oil into a steep-sided frying pan and place over a high heat while you cut out the doughnuts. Roll out the dough on a lightly floured surface. Cut to rings using a biscuit cutter and use a much smaller one to make the hole in the middle of each. Fry the doughnuts in batches in the hot oil for about 30 seconds on each side, using tongs to flip them over, before lifting out and draining on kitchen paper. Pour caster sugar onto a plate and gently dip the doughnuts in it to coat both sides while still warm.

Almond Macaroons

MAKES 16

Sweet treats often found their way into the picnic hamper, or were handed out liberally around the farmhouse table, but the Famous Five always finished their main course first. Mrs Beeton offers a recipe using ground almonds instead of flour, but the almond essence used here will provide plenty of flavour.

200g caster sugar
170g plain flour
60g ground almonds
½ tsp almond essence
60g butter, plus extra for greasing
1 tsp baking powder
2 egg whites
a few blanched almonds

Preheat the oven to 180°C/fan 160°C/350°F/gas 4, and grease and line a medium-size flat baking tray with parchment paper.

Combine all of the ingredients, except the blanched almonds, in a mixing bowl. Beat thoroughly with a wooden spoon. Spoon out golf ball-size pieces onto the prepared baking tray. Place a blanched almond on top of each macaroon and bake in the oven for 15 minutes or until golden brown.

Cherry Tart

SERVES 6

'And there's a cherry tart made with our own cherries, and our own cream with it. I know what hungry children are.'
(FIVE GO DOWN TO THE SEA)

In *Five Go Down to the Sea*, a cherry tart made with Mrs Penruthlan's own cherries is enough to set Dick smiling with pleasure.

FOR THE SWEET SHORTCRUST PASTRY BASE

225g plain flour
110g butter, plus extra for greasing
50g caster sugar
1 egg

FOR THE FILLING

500g cherries
50g butter
50g caster sugar
1 egg
3 drops of vanilla essence
50g ground almonds
icing sugar, for dusting

Preheat the oven to 190°C/fan 170°C/375°F/gas 5 and grease a large flan dish.

First, make the pastry. Sift the flour into a mixing bowl and rub in the butter. Add the sugar and work through with your fingers. Beat the egg, add it to the bowl and combine using a wooden spoon to form a dough. Roll out the dough on a floured surface and use it to line the greased flan dish. Prick the bottom well with a fork and leave in the fridge for 30 minutes. Line the pastry with parchment paper and weigh it down with dried peas or baking beads. Blind bake the pastry case in the oven for 10–15 minutes until pale golden.

For the filling, halve the cherries using a paring knife and remove the stones. Cream the butter and sugar together in a bowl. Beat the egg and add to the bowl with the vanilla essence and ground almonds.

Mix until smooth. When the pastry base is ready, fill it with the almond mixture and cover with the halved cherries, cut side down. Press the cherries a little way into the filling and bake in the oven for 20 minutes.

Allow to cool and dust with icing sugar before serving.

'Meat pies, fruit pies, hams, a great round tongue, pickles, sauces, jam tarts, stewed and fresh fruit, jellies, a great trifle, jugs of cream – there was no end to the things Mrs Penruthlan had got ready. She laughed when she saw the children peeping there and marvelling.'
(FIVE GO DOWN TO THE SEA)

Trifle

SERVES 4

If it weren't for the Famous Five *trifling* in the affairs of ne'er-do-wells, the country would be overrun with crooks and villains, so this dessert seems particularly apt. Of course, the bananas would not have been available to our Famous friends; consider them a modern-day luxury.

4 trifle sponges
sweet sherry
2 bananas
440g fresh strawberries

FOR THE CUSTARD
275ml double cream
3 egg yolks
25g caster sugar
1 tsp cornflour

FOR THE TOPPING
300ml double cream
50g lightly toasted flaked almonds

Break up the trifle sponges and lay them in the bottom of a trifle or big glass bowl. Soak with a glug of sweet sherry. Peel and slice the bananas and arrange over the sponge. Wash and hull the strawberries, then halve and arrange over the sliced banana.

Prepare the custard by heating the cream in a saucepan. Mix the egg yolks, sugar and cornflour in a bowl with a little of the cream then add to the saucepan with the rest of the cream. Simmer very gently, stirring with a wooden spoon until the custard thickens. Remove from heat and allow to cool.

Spread the custard over the fruit in the trifle bowl and level off with a palette knife or a spatula.

Whip the double cream for the topping until thick then spread evenly over the surface of the trifle and scatter with the almonds. Put the trifle in the fridge for a couple of hours to set.

'There was nothing for Timmy to drink except home-made lemonade, and he didn't seem to like that very much.'
(FIVE GO DOWN TO THE SEA)

Chapter Five

LASHINGS OF DELICIOUS DRINKS

'"Really?" said Julian, pouring himself out a third lemonade.'
(FIVE GO DOWN TO THE SEA)

Lemonade

MAKES 2 GLASSES

Home-made lemonade – there's nothing quite like it on a hot summer's day. It's certainly very popular with Julian, Dick, Anne and George – they seem to down a glass in lots of the stories.

1 unwaxed lemon, plus extra slices to serve
1 tbsp sugar
6 ice cubes, plus extra to serve
700ml cold water

Chop the lemon into pieces and place all of the ingredients in a blender and whizz. Strain into a jug and serve with extra ice and a slice of lemon.

Lime Juice

MAKES ABOUT 500ML

'"Very kind of you. But I've had an enormous tea," said Mr Luffy. "I've brought up a fruit cake for you, from my own larder. Shall we share it for supper? And I've got a bottle of lime juice, too, which will taste grand with some of the stream water."'
(FIVE GO OFF TO CAMP)

With all the sunshine and vitamin C a child could ever need, it's a fairly safe bet that neither, Julian, Dick, George or Anne ever suffered from rickets or scurvy. A cool, refreshing glass of lime juice in the summer sun is enough to quench the thirst of any adventurer.

10 limes
300g caster sugar
1 tsp citric acid
fizzy water, to serve

YOU WILL NEED
1 x 500ml sterilised bottle (see page 26)
pestle and mortar

Remove the peel from the fruit using a vegetable peeler, taking care not to cut away any of the pith. Chop the peel and set aside.

Halve the peeled limes and extract the juice into a bowl. Stir in the sugar and citric acid, and keep stirring until all of the sugar has dissolved.

Crush the chopped peel with a pestle and mortar to release the oils and add to the juice.

Cover with clingfilm and leave to steep for 24 hours. Strain through a sieve and pour into a sterilised bottle. Dilute with fizzy water to serve.

Orangeade

MAKES 8 GLASSES

'The little shop sold lemonade, orangeade, lime juice, grapefruit juice and ginger beer. It was really difficult to choose which to have.'
(FIVE GET INTO TROUBLE)

A fine refreshing drink served over ice and diluted slightly with fizzy water.

200ml water
100g sugar
8 oranges
½ lemon

TO SERVE
fizzy water
ice cubes

Warm the water in a saucepan and add the sugar to form a syrup. Stir until the sugar has completely dissolved. Zest and juice the oranges and add to the syrup along with the juice of the half-lemon and stir well.

Transfer to a jug. Allow to cool completely then refrigerate. Serve diluted to taste with fizzy water over ice. If you don't manage to drink it all, the orangeade will keep overnight in the fridge.

Ginger Beer

MAKES ABOUT 3 LITRES

It's what the Famous Five are famous for these days, drinking 'lashings of ginger beer'. Interestingly, Enid Blyton never actually used the word 'lashings' to describe the amount of ginger beer the Five were getting through. There were lashings of boiled eggs and lashings of radishes, but never lashings of ginger beer. The phrase comes from a spoof film made for TV, called *Five Go Mad in Dorset*.

20g root ginger, peeled
500g sugar
juice and rind of 1 lemon
15g cream of tartar
3 litres boiling water
15g brewer's yeast

YOU WILL NEED
6 x 500ml sterilised glass bottles with stoppers *(see page 26)*

Wrap the root ginger in a tea towel and wallop it with a rolling pin to bruise it well. Place it, the sugar, the juice and rind of the lemons and the cream of tartar in a large heatproof glass mixing bowl. Pour over the boiling water and cover with a tea towel. Allow to cool until lukewarm.

Next, stir in the yeast. Re-cover the bowl with a cloth and allow to brew at room temperature overnight. In the morning, skim any yeast from the surface and carefully decant into sterilised glass bottles with ceramic swing-top stoppers. Leave for 3 days in a cool dark place, after which the ginger beer will be ready to drink.

'They all felt better when they were eating the sandwiches and drinking the ginger beer'
(FIVE ON A TREASURE ISLAND)

'Anne began to plan what she would give the little company for supper. Ham, certainly – and tomatoes – and some of that raspberry syrup diluted with icy-cold spring-water.'
(FIVE GO OFF IN A CARAVAN)

Raspberry Syrup

MAKES ROUGHLY ½ LITRE

This sweet, sticky syrup is delicious poured over ice and diluted with spring water, either fizzy or still. It also works well as a treat if you pour, just a little, over vanilla ice cream or perhaps even over a cream cake.

500g raspberries
500ml water
200g sugar

YOU WILL NEED
sterilised bottle (see *page 26)*

Wash the raspberries and place in a large saucepan with the water. Bring to the boil, then turn down the heat and simmer for 20 minutes.

Once the raspberries have broken down and lost their colour, pour through a sieve into a clean smaller pan. Discard the fruit pulp.

Add the sugar to the juice and bring to a rolling boil. Boil until all the sugar has dissolved and the liquid has reduced by about a third. Pour into a sterilised glass bottle and seal immediately. The syrup will keep in a dark, cool place for up to a month, but store in the fridge once opened.

'"I think some hot cocoa would do us all good," said Aunt Fanny.'
(FIVE GO TO SMUGGLER'S TOP)

A Cup of Cocoa

SERVES 4 (THE DOG CAN LICK THE (COOL) PAN!)

Here's a recipe to make as you gather with your three favourite (and possibly famous) friends, a last snack before you settle down for the night ahead of tomorrow's adventures.

70g unsweetened cocoa powder
150g golden caster sugar
100ml water
900ml whole milk

In a medium saucepan, mix the cocoa powder and sugar with a few splashes of the water or milk and cream together to make a smooth paste. Slowly add the rest of the liquid, making sure there are no lumps.

Turn on the heat and bring to the boil, then turn down the heat and simmer for a couple of minutes. Pour into four large mugs and gather around the campfire.

Elderflower Syrup

MAKES ABOUT 3 LITRES

The English hedgerows are awash with elderflower in June, and this quintessential English cordial recipe is jolly simple to make.

25–30 heads of elderflower blossom
2kg granulated sugar
3 litres boiling water
3 unwaxed lemons
75g citric acid
fizzy water, to serve

YOU WILL NEED
3 x 1l sterilised bottles (see page 26)
a muslin cloth

Wash off the flower heads, checking to remove any wildlife. Place the sugar in a large stockpot and pour over the boiling water, giving it a good stir to help the sugar dissolve.

Slice the lemons and add them to the sugar solution along with the citric acid. Then add the flower heads, cover with clingfilm and leave to steep for 24 hours.

Strain through a muslin cloth in a sieve and decant into three sterilised bottles.

To drink, dilute with fizzy water.

Acknowledgements

An absolutely wizard, and top hole thanks to my children Ruby and Wilf, for giving me the idea to write this book. A nod and a wink to Sarah L, who spurred me on and fired me up, and three jolly massive cheers for Emily Barrett and Lorraine Jerram, who together with the amazing illustrators, Ruth Palmer and Emanuel Santos, made it all happen.

About the Authors

JOSH SUTTON is a freelance writer and illustrator with a focus on food and travel. He is a member of the Guild of Food Writers and the author of three books. Josh writes and illustrates a regular column in *Camping Magazine* and *STIR to Action* magazine. His words and pictures have appeared in the *Guardian*, the *Yorkshire Post, Coast Magazine, Country Walking* and *Scotland Outdoors.* He is also a Famous Five aficionado and has previously been interviewed on the *One Show* regarding his *Guardian* article, 'Why the Famous Five had the perfect austerity diet'.

About the Authors

ENID BLYTON is one of the world's bestselling children's authors. Sales of her books are in excess of 500 million copies, and they have been translated into over 40 languages. Enid Blyton began her career as a school teacher before becoming a bestselling children's book author, writing over 800 books and stories. In 2017, she was the UK's 12th biggest-selling children's author, selling a book every two minutes, and appeared in the top ten of The 50 Greatest Storytellers of All Time (Canon UK). As well as being regularly voted the UK's best-loved author, Enid Blyton is the most translated children's author in the world according to UNESCO, and many of her books have been adapted into films and TV series. Her most popular series include: *The Famous Five, The Secret Seven, The Naughtiest Girl, The Adventure Series, The Magic Faraway Tree, St Clare's* and *Malory Towers.*

Further Reading

Those interested in some further reading may enjoy the following titles:

Beeton, I., *Beeton's Dictionary of Everyday Cookery* (London, 1900).

Collingham, L., *The Taste of War – World War Two and the Battle for Food* (London, 2012).

Colquhoun, K., *Taste – The Story of Britain through its Cooking* (London, 2007).

Craig, E., *Simple Cooking* (London, 1934).

Hix, M., *British Food* (London, 2005).

Jopson, M., *The Science of Food – An exploration of what we eat and how we cook* (London, 2017).

Nash, E., *Cooking Craft* (London, 1931).

Slater, N., *Eating for England – The Delights & Eccentricities of the British at Table* (London, 2007).

Index

R

T

V

W

Books in The Famous Five series

1. Five On a Treasure Island
2. Five Go Adventuring Again
3. Five Run Away Together
4. Five Go to Smuggler's Top
5. Five Go Off in a Caravan
6. Five On Kirrin Island Again
7. Five Go Off to Camp
8. Five Get Into Trouble
9. Five Fall Into Adventure
10. Five on a Hike Together
11. Five Have a Wonderful Time
12. Five Go Down to the Sea
13. Five Go to Mystery Moor
14. Five Have Plenty of Fun
15. Five on a Secret Trail
16. Five Go to Billycock Hill
17. Five Get Into a Fix
18. Five on Finniston Farm
19. Five Go to Demon's Rocks
20. Five Have a Mystery to Solve
21. Five Are Together Again

Jolly Good Food

A children's cookbook packed with simple and delicious recipes inspired by Enid Blyton's stories. If you or your family have ever wanted to eat google buns with Moonface in the Magic Faraway Tree or indulge in a midnight feast with the girls of Malory Towers, this full-colour book with recipes by acclaimed chef, restauranteur, TV presenter and mum, Allegra McEvedy, will be the perfect treat.

Hodder Children's Books £14.99

'"My word, why don't people always have meals like this?"'
(FIVE RUN AWAY TOGETHER)